To: B [D0334864]

on his ordination to

the Priesthood

at Petertide 1978

in

Liverpool Cathedral

Philippians Chapter 1 verse 5.

Graeme Spiers

———

Freedom, Suffering and Love

FREEDOM, SUFFERING AND LOVE

Andrew Elphinstone

SCM PRESS LTD

334 00502 7
First published 1976
by SCM Press Ltd
58 Bloomsbury Street, London
© SCM Press Ltd 1976
Printed in Great Britain by
W & J Mackay Limited,
Chatham

CONTENTS

There are more things in heaven and earth
than the condemnation of man,
and more in the coming of Christ
than the lifting of that condemnation.

FOREWORD

I owe the writing of this book to a great many people and a great many events in my life. The psychologists tell us that it is in the very early years that there begins the process of working out the inter-relationship between happiness and unhappiness, approval and disapproval, fulfilments and deprivation of desire, love and hate, pain and pleasure, and that this infantile and post-infantile calculation forms the basis of what should become the ability to make the mature assessments and responsible judgments of adult life. Childhood is seldom as happy as adult optimists make it out to be, and often it is markedly more full of stress than they realize. Working things out may for some temperaments become a habit, and if it is, through inclination and environment, strongly established, it continues through life and its owner may not be content until he or she has come to the encounter with larger matters like the suffering of man, the love of God and the suffering of Christ.

In particular, however, I owe it to certain individuals. To Bishop Stephen Neill, who long ago and often against my will spent endless energies bringing me into the active practice of the Christian faith – energies for which at the time I was not sufficiently grateful. To Professor G. R. Dunstan who, as Editor of *Theology*, asked me to write one of a series of articles in which some of these ideas were first (and not very well) explored.[1] To the then Dean of Westminster, the Very Reverend Eric Abbott, who generously invited me to conduct the Three Hours Service

[1] 'Priesthood and the Tension between Christ and the World', *Theology* LXXI, April 1968, reprinted in *The Sacred Ministry*, ed. G. R. Dunstan, SPCK 1970.

in Westminster Abbey on Good Friday 1969, when these ideas were more deeply thought out and more clearly expressed. And to Mrs Charles Leach, neighbour and friend, who has not only encouraged me to proceed but has typed and retyped draft after draft – of this and other writings – until the tally of pages has become uncountable.

I am not going to say, as writers often do, that I owe it to the encouragement or long-suffering of my wife. That is because she has put up with worse things and more difficult times than this and has done so valiantly and with love. An effort of this kind is an exceedingly exacting preoccupation over a matter of years and cannot fail to affect the life of a household. She has certainly longed for it to be finished, and this has been an extra spur to progress and to completion.

ANDREW ELPHINSTONE

EDITOR'S NOTE

ANDREW ELPHINSTONE was born on Armistice Day 1918, the second son of Lord and Lady Elphinstone. His mother was a sister to Queen Elizabeth the Queen Mother. He spent his young life at the family home, Carberry Tower, near Musselburgh. He was educated at Eton and New College, Oxford, where he was reading PPE when war broke out in 1939. He was called up with the Cameron Highlanders but, as a result of heart trouble while at school, he was never passed fit for active service. He went as ADC to the Viceroy of India from 1940 to 1943, and while thus employed he learned Urdu, a language in which he became quite proficient. On his return to England he worked in the Intelligence Section of the War Office until demobilization in 1946.

In 1948 Andrew entered Wycliffe Hall, Oxford, to read theology. He was ordained in Salisbury Cathedral on St Thomas's Day 1950, and he served his curacy at Wimborne Minster until 1953. Then he became Rector of Worplesdon until, after nine years, ill health forced him to resign.

Andrew was a very enthusiastic person, endowed with many gifts, and among them a very active mind. He threw himself whole-heartedly into everything he did: gardening and psychology, languages and music (he was an above average pianist), archaeology and ethnology. His intense interest in people was heightened by his parochial ministry, and his ability as a patient listener and wise counsellor – always generous in his courtesy – endeared him to persons of all ages and all walks of life.

All these gifts he brought with him when he acted as host to a series of small theological working parties convened, on his invitation, by the staff of the Advisory Council for the Church's Ministry at Glenmazaran, in Inverness-shire. The most notable of these resulted in the publication of *Teaching Christian Ethics* by SCM Press in 1974. It was at one of these that I first met Andrew in 1967, and heard him, in walks up the glen, turning over in his mind the ideas which have become this book.

How he first gave these ideas form he has told in his own Foreword to the book. Thereafter he did not cease to work on them. Drafts of every paragraph were written, dated, copied, re-written, re-copied, re-arranged, some many times. His perfectionism, seen in him as a gardener and musician, showed itself also in words. The last pieces were dated March 1975. When he died, on the nineteenth day of that month, the work must have been approaching what he wanted it to be; but the final revision and ordering of the parts were incomplete. I have tried to fulfil his intention, so far as I could discern it, with the lightest editorial hand.

'... il capo chino
tenea, come uom che reverente vada.'

Easter 1976   G. R. DUNSTAN

❧ I ☙

The Bundle to be Untied

THIS IS A religious book, a book about Christianity; but it is no kind of devotional manual for the piously inclined. That is the last thing it is.

Its purpose is to show that the present primacy of pain and unrest in the world is part of the raw material of the ultimate primacy of love. This is contained within another wider purpose, which is to make a full acknowledgment that our furthest ancestors – and therefore ourselves – are creatures arisen through evolution from an origin in a vastly distant past. Wiser men than I, and more learned ones, have long been doubting the proposition that there existed an innocence which was destroyed by a culpable disaster on man's part. Anthropology has long suggested that there was no height from which to fall, no perfection to disrupt, no relationship with the Creator to break, no tested morality to flout. All was originally primitive, all in a state of growing and of gradual evolutionary becoming. Thereby hangs a tale of great significance for Christianity, which will deepen its foundations and strengthen its orthodoxy.

I have in mind people who are deeply convinced about their faith but still feel in a muddle about their own lives and their own responses to God. People who stick valiantly to their religious practice without really understanding for sure where this will lead, or whether it leads anywhere beyond the fulfilment of duty, but who have been brought up in that way and do not like to deviate from it. People who have tried to find validity and truth in Christianity and have, for one reason or another, given up the struggle; or who have weighed Christianity in the balance (a private balance and not often the right one) and found it wanting and have gone to hunt for some other religion or for some more exotic brand of spirituality. And those people, for whom I feel strongly, who have rejected Christianity sincerely and even passionately because the version of it which has come their way by upbringing or insipid presentation in church has failed to satisfy the largeness of truth and generosity of spirit which they rightly looked for.

I am writing for some of the more elderly who see little hope in the future and who think that the good and delightful world they once knew is gone to the dogs or at least is heading for disaster: and for the younger people who feel with passion that the older generations have been culpable in failing to make the world what it might be and certainly ought to be. And it is also, therefore, for the indignant who are outraged at the state of society and shocked at the ineffectualness of the church and who think that the last thing in the world which could ever bring a solution to any problem is Christianity.

The book is addressed also to fellow-clergymen, and it does not matter of what allegiance. These are not things over which denominations are disagreed. Clergymen are largely in the same predicament wherever they are. More than anyone else they have to meet the wonders and share the worries of the unhappy, the disillusioned and the indignant. Often they find themselves at a loss to satisfy the hungry soul with the traditional teaching they have learnt or with the insight they themselves gained within the limitations of that teaching. If this brings any enlargement of vision to their enormously delicate task, it will have served part of its purpose.

It is addressed also to that much more learned body of people who constitute the official theological world. Since it is concerned with pain and love and forgiveness, with the fact of freedom and the problem of evil, it is offered as a contribution to what in these circles is known as the doctrine of atonement. This is far from being an academic or a scholarly book, and academics and scholars may perhaps, from time to time, think that such a book needs to be written. Furthermore, partly because it is written for ordinary people and partly because writers ought to be able to express the truth they see in ordinary words, this book does not use that technical religious terminology which baffles the ordinary reader and which, it may be confessed, sometimes relieves the writer of the job of explaining what he really means in terms of day-to-day language. In these days, when a lot of things appear to be going wrong in the world, when violence and wickedness seem to be flourishing, it is more than ever important to delve further into what Christianity is able to say about the meaning of unrest, the significance of suffering and the beckoning horizon of love. This is something which is urgently needed for a bewildered generation and it is needed right across all the boundaries of denomination.

No doubt the living of human life has always been and will continue to be a highly exacting and baffling business. No doubt it will be interspersed with only occasional shafts of insight and occasional moments of the quiescence which follows achievement. There seems little doubt that this is in fact the way the Creator desires things to be because of the single over-riding object for which he desires to create. Human personality is the crowning achievement of creation, and the forming of it depends to a large extent on the searching, the experiencing and the endeavouring which it is forced to undertake in such things as the weighing of moral cause and effect, the meeting of opposition and adversity, and not least the searching for the reality of God who purposely does not make the perceiving of himself an easy or effortless affair. Behind the scenes of our existence, the outward facade of each person, far profounder creative activity is at work than we may often be aware of, and the hazard, caprice and uncertainty make a *milieu* in which special and indeed unique quality is being produced. The ideas which have haunted the thinking of some idealists, philosophers and politicians, and which have pulled at the heart-strings of men and women through the ages, that mankind has a right to a smooth and painless passage in life and a right to resent as an evil and an outrage whatever ruffles the external calm, are wishful thinkings which set the human target at far too mean a level, quite out of touch with the reality which is the arena of our endeavouring. A utopian orderliness or a cellophane-wrapped existence might be a groundwork for producing some kind of conscious being, but certainly not the kind which God has desired and designed.

If the world really is primarily the arena of mankind's making above all other things, then the hazards and uncertainties of our existence become understandable. Freedom is a very dynamic condition for things to happen in: love a very dynamic thing to want – and to be promised. Suffering is inseparable from both, but it is also a very dynamic thing in the forming of man's spirit and it turns out to be the single most important human experience. Probably the world cannot be much other than it is with all its intensities of happiness and of suffering. Here in this turbulence is every element which could possibly be required for the forming of humankind and, in humankind by God's grace, of character, personality and spirit. And if we go a step further, it is in this roughness of environment that the gifts of the Holy Spirit – wisdom, understanding, fortitude, temperance, spiritual strength – are given to whoever pursues the search for God through thick and thin and therefore steps further than most over the threshold of love.

The forming of a physical world (this or any other in the universe) must have been a series of violent and sometimes terrifying processes. By analogy, the forming of human personality, from smallest biological origin to something sufficiently splendid to be what religion calls God-likeness, must be of still more formidable creative significance. What we are ourselves seeing and taking part in is the continuing act of God's creation, no longer at a physical level but at a spiritual, of which the raw materials are the more vulnerable and explosive ones of human feeling, thought, emotion and will. There need be no surprise if this latter phase of

creation contains a climax of turbulence (and of magnificence
still half-hidden), and no surprise if God in person takes part at
first hand. What is on the anvil is not mountains and seas but men
and women, being made for kinship with God, with a capacity
for sharing his creative imagination, his dimension of freedom and
his depth of love. Mountains and seas may be created from 'outside' but men and women from 'within'. It is certainly not man's
littleness nor is it wholly man's wickedness which accounts for
the world's apparent topsy-turviness. The meaning of our unrest
is to be discovered in the greatness of man's destiny and in man's
strange uniqueness amid all that has been created. Alone in his
position as man he must undergo a transformation, a metamorphosis, an alchemy in which all his array of earth-born
qualities have to be re-created into the qualities of eternity. It is
not impossible to suppose that the whole created universe exists
for this purpose and is clustered round this happening. Even if the
same thing is taking place in other planets (as well it may), the
same qualities must distinguish the participants. No longer animals (certainly no naked ape or human zoo-man): not angels
because of the possession of flesh, blood and freedom: as far from
God as from the animal world: yet having urge, aspiration and
capacity to be like God, higher than angels, partaking of divine
nature. And this all arising out of the lowliness of flesh, blood and
freedom.

Christianity has never been sure of itself in balancing the two
aspects of man's being, the earth-born and the heaven-bent, the
noble and the ignoble, the uniquely privileged and the equally
specially condemned. On one side is the intense concern for man
and for human life which has (though one may have forgotten
this) been responsible for much of the impetus behind social
service, medicine, education and even science and technology.
On the other side is the acknowledgment of man's baseness and
evil. Christianity does not go along with the poet's condemnation
that amid all the natural loveliness of things 'only man is vile'. But
it has tended to have a condemnatory view of man, emphazising

his sinfulness, his nothingness or his transitoriness. The credibility gap which some feel to lie between the church and the world may be caused partly by the hunch that Christian faith is loaded too heavily on the pessimistic side and is not imparting a real or worthy symptom of what man is. Surprisingly, to the rescue of Christianity in this respect comes a scientific discipline to give a fresh largeness to our vision of man and a disentanglement of the threads of his conduct and, most important, of his culpability. We can see man in his reality as an evolutionary creature and not as he appears through lenses of myth and legend.

Wiser men than I have long since understood that the opening chapters of Genesis, with the familiar stories of the creation and of the disobedience in Eden, are not accounts of historical events. They could not possibly, by any stretch of the imagination, be so. They are ancient myth and legend, although certainly myth and legend which remain alive with true insights about man's spiritual condition and reactions. A hundred and more years have gone by since the theory of evolution began to be accepted, and it is a hundred also since Old Testament scholars did their own disentangling of the source of those chapters, and separated historical fact from spiritual legend. Man, we can now say without a shred of doubt, did not come ready-made from the hand of God in some perfect Eden. He arose through a long dramatic process of evolution and came to manhood after untold trials, errors and struggles, equipped with a powerful array of arms and armour – aggressive, defensive, self-protective – with which evolution furnished him while he moved towards his intellectual and psychic dominance. This in fact makes man a more realistic subject for Christian understanding. His freedom is more real, his suffering more fundamental, his love, when it kindles, of more value. The erstwhile portrait of man born in mythical perfection with clear-cut instructions about good and evil, who then consciously chose evil, is a long way away from the true picture we know of unconscious drive, mixed motive and over-powering passion.

I have entitled this book *Freedom, Suffering and Love* because I believe that these are the principal ingredients of man's development and the principal signposts pointing us towards the meaning of man's existence. It is (I need hardly say) my own conviction that the account which Christianity gives of man is the only valid one. The way in which I want to trace the force of that validity is by discussing these three things – and others – which are of human experiencing and of very great human importance. They lead me to a more profound grasp of the meaning of Christ's coming, living and suffering than by approaching it the other way. Most Christian apologists start with questions about man's immorality in order to show the purpose of Christ's sufferings. This order of things I find falls on deaf ears, and my own are included. We are too conditioned to seeing Christ as the antidote to man's wickedness for it to remain meaningful. But freedom, suffering and love are existential and meaningful things and, coupled with the flood of light thrown on man's make-up and situation in the world by the idea of evolution, they appear to make sense of what, to many, had become senseless. This book is no opium of the people. It will arouse suspicions in the hearts of some faithful defenders of the *status quo*, who may think that it plays fast and loose with Holy Scripture. But trees which are healthy bend with the wind yet remain upright; they grow new branches and let old ones die; and all the while their roots go deeper. Christianity is very healthy and can take new things in its stride, be buffeted by them and yet thrive on the experience. If it were not so it would not contain universal truth about God's creation and his creative intent. And that is exactly what it does contain.

What has enthralled me most in the long process of thinking out and working out the argument of this book is that, starting as I do from an evolutionary standpoint about man and looking particularly at the three mainstays of freedom, suffering and love, there has emerged the fact (emerged is correct because I did not try to organize it so) that the activity which we call forgiveness occupies the central position in a discussion of man as God-made in freedom and God-destined through love. This is surely a hint of validity from the Christian point of view. By forgiveness I do not mean exclusively the forgiveness of man by God. Christianity has tended to lay so much emphasis on this cardinal necessity in Christian faith that it has laid too little on the other aspect of forgiveness, that of one human by another. Christ made this quite central in the Lord's Prayer, '. . . as we forgive them that trespass against us', and in other parts of his teaching. It seems to emerge that forgiveness in both its directions is the instrument by which the defeat of the devil is brought about, and furthermore that the forgiveness of man by man is in no way far behind that of man by God as the instrument of man's liberation. People can hardly believe at first hearing that it can be so, for forgiveness is sometimes seen as affecting small things in which not much sacrifice is required in order to forgive. But it is in fact the most exacting exercise of love in the whole field of human relationship.

Forgiveness brings us face to face with pain, for, whatever else it is made up of, it is centrally the matter of dealing with pain; if you have not been hurt there is nothing to forgive. That is why it is the most exacting exercise of love. The vital thing which evolution tells us is that pain lies at the heart of that massive array of equipments which have ensured man's survival and advance. Man's vulnerability is his safeguard, and it is also the trigger for his aggressiveness, defensiveness and will to dominate – and his refusal to forgive. Thus it is that evil is enabled to proliferate and that a vicious circle of hurt, counter-hurt and yet more hurt drives people and groups further apart until they cease to see each other's need or the validity of each other's point of view at all. Pain is indeed the single most significant experience of humanity.

It need not, however, be destructive or divisive; it need not proliferate or form vicious circles. What Christ was doing, in innermost meaning, in the crucifixion was to accomplish the dealing with pain in such a way that it could not be any of these things. In him love rose to its climax in meeting pain and in-

justice, to its most totally exacting dimension, and remained unbroken. That is forgiveness, because whom you go on loving you
do not any more even desire to condemn or revenge yourself
upon. So man's forgiveness was assured but, almost as vital, the
trail of man's forgiveness of man was blazed. The evil of man's
proliferating estrangements was shown to be terminable.

That laid before man the challenge to enter the exercise of love
in this highest dimension. That entry into such a love requires
absolutely the power of divine grace without which man succumbs
before the instinct of self-protection and revenge. That forgiveness defeats evil and the love which powers it is the foundation of
man's own growing in likeness to God.

The second thing which enthralled me was to follow the
strange course of the function of love; and here again evolution
has brought quite a new perspective to this understanding. We
have been accustomed – because of the old ready-made idea from
Genesis from which we have not really shaken free – to think of
the human race as having always possessed the fundamental
characteristics of love, fear, vulnerability to pain, hate, selfishness
and so forth. These things have been regarded as existing in a
bundle alongside each other and as being the criteria of goodness
or badness, righteousness or sinfulness, morality or immorality.
True enough: sin is man's failure in love towards God or his
neighbour. But love is no more ready-made than was man, either
racially or individually. Love was a latecomer in the story: in its
aspect of love for neighbour or love for God, a very latecomer
indeed, learned with blood, sweat and tears over many centuries.
The Old Testament is largely the story of that long, slow, reluc-
tant lesson: and it was not completed until the life of Christ
showed its full and final dimension. It was he who said 'A new
commandment I give unto you, that ye love one another as I have
loved you', and the human race had been the human race since
far mistier antiquity than that.

Pain is incomparably more ancient, much more deeply indigenous to human experience. Religious teaching says that love

is the deepest reality in life and that man is expected to show love uppermost in his conduct. But love is 'a new commandment', as Christ said, and almost everything he said and did out of love courted opposition, derision and persecution. It was too new, too unexpected, too much against the grain of that great tide of evolutionary instinct with which man is filled. Pain is deeper, more to be feared than love is desired, surrounded by its panoplies of self-defence, self-interest, the will to survive. Love is the herald of the end, embryo of eternity, quality of the new creation in the likeness of God, characteristic of the freedom to which we are beckoned. We have come to the threshold of this love, and we find it a strange and exacting *milieu* to be in. But we are in it, for it came with the chosen race and confronted us to the full in Christ. We cannot pretend we are not in it: the fact that we are is part of the meaning of our unrest. Love is not only new, it has more alarming implications than simply newness.

The human race stands at the end of a prodigious climb on the evolutionary slopes – one might equally say a long struggle through the evolutionary jungle. Perhaps in some ways, like adaptation to modern environments, we may still be evolving, because the process is deeply in-built. But in all important respects evolution is finished, man's intellectual dominance and conscious powers have long been established. Evolution is no longer his prime necessity in order to be truly man. That phase of his development is over. Now the new and more subtle challenge faces him: the demand of love. This is no invention of religious systems, no Christian wool pulled over the eyes. Evolution itself, bringing man to more advanced psychological refinement, brought the dawn of it. Justice and law advanced its scope; man's 'feeling after' God lifted the social exercise of neighbourly love into a spiritual obligation owed to God; and man was launched on his religious quest of love.

But love, when it came upon man's horizon, turned out to be a revolutionary task-master requiring the capitulation of unit after unit of the evolutionary equipment so painstakingly built up for

man's survival. Love is open and yields up its defences; it holds
back aggression, giving more than receiving; it bears pain and
does not take revenge. It is, from a worldly angle, madness, nonsense and suicide. It challenges all our evolutionary instincts and
requires, if not their annihilation, then at least their transformation.
It brought crucifixion once in known circumstances and it brings
it a million million times in less cosmic but intimately poignant
ones for individuals. Men and women resist the demands of love
with all their might because so much of their might is evolutionary,
survivalist, of nature and not yet of supernature. But its logic is
undeniable and increasing since the world and society become
progressively more turbulent. Politics, economics, science, technology do not provide panaceas. Organized religion often does
not, but what is concealed at the heart of it but so dreadfully
absent sometimes is love, the bearing of pain, the forgiveness
which cures evil's proliferation: this can answer turbulence, and
man is being steadily driven towards discovering it as the solvent
of ills.

Evolution with its equipments and vulnerabilities has to be
transformed, transposed into another key, alchemized, used as
raw material. (Religion says simply, and effectively, redeemed.)
Central to this transformation is the old enemy and friend of man,
pain. When religion says that Christ suffered for our sins, it does
not say enough. I repeat that forgiveness does not cease to be
central, and in establishing love's supremacy over every circumstance and every infliction Christ forged out the inner meaning of
forgiveness because, for ever, love would not and could not fail
or be deflected. But in so doing he, the man of evolution (as I shall
call him later), took into himself the whole brunt and power of
evolution, and of the pain which is its spinal nerve, and turned it
into means of spirit and God-likeness.

Some of my friends who have heard the gist of what follows
have asked me whether the argument might not be as cogent, and
more acceptable for some, if it did not bring in the devil or demon,
whichever word one may use. I cannot visualize it without the

place in it which the devil occupies. Someone else may do this, but not I. My basic difficulty is that I do actually believe that the devil, spiritual master-mind of anti-God, does exist and it would be silly (and false) to write as though I did not so believe. The evidence for his reality is, to me, overwhelming even if only because God's task and our lot in life would surely be more simple if he did not exist. I think Utopia might have come, but I think that man's spiritual dimension would be a mean second-best. The argument, I fear, must be taken as it stands and I believe that on the whole more people will find it real with the devil included than unreal.

৵ 2 ৶

Pain Abundant, Love Seeming Scarce

WHEN THEY DARE to allow themselves to think, the ordinary man and the ordinary woman must often feel lost among the mixture of reason and unreason in the world around them. If so, they are not the only ones to be baffled at the meaning of what is happening. Those who are appointed as the exponents of Christianity, who are themselves basically ordinary people, are not without their share of the same experience. They have to embrace a much wider and more difficult range of explanations than was once the case if they are to give an account of the times in which we live. They also have had some of their familiar signposts withdrawn and find themselves in new and exacting uncertainties.

The age of unquestioning faith has, for many people in the Western world, long since gone and for others it is fast going. The church has seen the yielding up of almost all the areas of control which were once its sole prerogative. It has seen the taking over by the state of medical care and education, and it has seen the secularization of compassion towards the needy. In public discussion on many subjects the voice of Christian religion is often not invited and therefore it generally goes unheard. Christianity has taken second, or even third or fourth place in the scale of importance in public affairs. Science is the rising, or risen, star, and politics, economics and sociology are all looked upon as the more practical and important ways of solving the problems of today.

This is not to be regretted, and it has come about assuredly by divine permission. It is also easily understandable at a time when the quest of secular knowledge and of technological advance has been the order of the day; when medical science has enabled well-nigh miraculous things to happen and when the frontiers of knowledge stretch from the universe around us to the smallest mechanisms supporting life within us. Out of the march of events, unfamiliar or painful though they may seem to be to the inherited framework of religion, new things always come. The age of unquestioning faith was a time perhaps of not enough questioning, and of a faith not required or expected to be understood in the mind of the believer. It was a time when the appointed exponent of religion could rely on an authoritarianism which he could wield by right without always an impeccable understanding in his own heart. For that, the divine permission has been and is being signally withdrawn. What he says now is analysed as never previously, often argued against and as often disbelieved. The days through which we are living require and are bringing to birth a ruggeder and a more penetrating spirit in Christian faith.

The ordinary person is pulled hither and thither between the magnetism of an inherited faith and an inherited morality on one side, and on the other the lure of a future in which secular answers are given to all questions and secular moralities made respectable. In this conflict of forces people are hard put to know whether to pay more heed to the white coat of science or to the black robe of religion. On the whole and for a majority of people it is probably the man in the white coat who is regarded as the prophet of today. The man in the black robe is suspected of being a purveyor of obsolete wares and of obscurantist ideas.

Nevertheless, behind the scenes when those men and women do their private thinking, and their even more private worrying and sorrowing, they begin once again to look for a wisdom and a comfort which lie beyond the scope of this-worldly solutions. They recognize intuitively that there are concerns of an ultimate nature which belong in the department of the man in the black robe and in which he alone is able to be the link-man to the level of truth they desire to find.

To suffer and to love are the two principal experiences of man's inward level of being, around which much of the drama of human life revolves. To these, as the title of this book suggests, must be added the partially neglected idea of freedom, because without it humanity, God, pain, love and life itself would all be equally inconceivable.

Suffering and love are things which go to make up much of what characterizes humanity as human. It is not to be wondered at if they are at the centre of the creative purpose. The divine purpose is concentrated on the unfolding of the human story. If it were not so, then Christ would not have become man, involving the divine intention in the toils of the human situation and infusing into the human status the seed of an embryonic divinity. Love and suffering are deeply indigenous to the ups and downs of human experience and they are therefore by the same token indigenous to the divine purpose. This, of course, the world has seen in the suffering of Christ and in the love which Christianity proclaims was proved and vindicated in it. Turning again to the ordinary man and woman, the love and the suffering which come their ways are, because of this, inextricably connected with what is contained in the purposes of God, and whether we like it or not we are in the midst of the dynamic of what God is doing in the world. We may feel at a loss amid the course of events, but it is in them, if we may but understand them, that the ultimate harmony of creation is being hammered out. We are irretrievably at the heart of the creative purpose because we are accessible to the influences and the infinite consequences of these two things; and fundamentally we do not desire to be retrieved from them.

When we talk of love, the meaning it usually has for us is of love in its human connotation: the love of man and woman or of parent and child, the attachment of kith and kin, the closeness of friends, the love of lovers. That aspect of love is true and splendid and is the thing for which people long above most other things – a many-splendoured thing indeed. It may be no coincidence that in some languages to live and to love are akin in word as they are in experience. Neither to receive love nor to have anyone to whom to give it (and the second may be more poignant than the first) is, of all situations, the most lonely and the most stultifying.

At the same time this human love is only a part of the whole dimension of love (if we believe that there does exist something more than purely human). It is not yet love in its complete or most durable form. It is still dependent on the whim of feeling; it can be turned away or turned off by anger, or changed to hate and revenge by disappointment. It can be mistaken for what is in effect infatuation and it can wither away and die. Even so, it is still the passport to human happiness, the inspiration to brave deeds and great art; and not least of its functions is to be a hint, a glimpse, an intimation, of something more splendid still which lies largely beyond our ken.

Of love in its widest sense, in what we must from now on call its divine dimension, grown beyond risk of damage and beyond the capriciousness of circumstance, we do not yet know very much, at least in our own experience. We may occasionally be aware of it in some moment of illumination, or we may be fortunate enough to see the authentic touch of its quality in the selflessness or forgiveness on the part of another person. We hear of its existence preached and exhorted by religion, but it can often seem a distant reality and hard to fit in with what we see around us. One of the greatest difficulties about the idea of divine love is the amount of human pain and suffering, and indeed animal suffering too, that is to be seen around us.

When we talk of pain or of suffering it brings to mind too readily the idea of bodily pain. Whichever word we use, whether pain or suffering, it must be taken as applying to every department of body or of feeling, inward even more than outward. In the mind of anyone who will read on, there is one thing which must be absolutely excluded from the beginning and that is the idea that pain means only physical or 'medical' pain. That would make nonsense of what follows and render the argument impenetrable because we are to be the more concerned with pain of feeling than we are with pain of body. Nature, dubbed as red in tooth and claw, is no doubt mostly aware of physical hurt (though has not fear a large part in animal suffering?). Mankind, red in heart and mind more than in tooth and claw, yet at the same time deeply vulnerable in inward feeling, is more at the mercy of all those pains which come from injustice, misunderstanding, the deprivation of love or the multiple variations of hurt feelings.

Pain we know all too well, more by far than we know about love. No part of it lies beyond our ken. It is with us and always has been with us, here and now, in every life, around every corner.

Here is a paradox and a problem which has exercised the thought of man throughout the ages and still teases the mind of professional thinker and of ordinary thinking person. Of pain, the thing we dread, there is such abundance; of love, the thing we desire, much seeming scarcity: and this in a world which has been created, so Christianity claims undeviatingly, by the God who is love!

This is one of the great questions on which people judge Christianity and on which its official exponents are challenged to give answers. The official exponent of Christianity, in whatever part of Christendom he may be appointed, besides the public services which some people believe to be his only obligation, has the more delicate task of interpreting God's purpose in the world and man's situation within it. He must place such crucial things as man's quest for love, his dread of suffering, his need of forgiveness, in their true perspective against the background of the divine purpose; for if he does not, no one else will. This is the province of religion, not of science or of politics or even of philosophy.

These things are matters both of contemporary and of perennial debate, and whatever other subjects devolve on to less specifically spiritual authorities, these remain central to religion. Christianity must grapple unremittingly with them, whether in private talk or in public discussion, because otherwise it risks being thought of as dealing only in the small change of religious affairs: a little comfort here, a little reproving there, some re-organizing of church services or of church government, some retranslation of liturgy and of scripture. Even the reunion of the churches can seem small coinage when the world is in pain and when the believing, let alone the unchurched, like hungry sheep look up for answers and have to confess themselves not always too well fed.

Those who have been brought up in the various portions of the Christian family learn the slants and the traditions of the particular part to which they belong. It is easy to know facts about other traditions, but it is scarcely possible for a person of one tradition to know what it feels like to be in another. This is true even when a change of allegiance has been made, since for the person in question the first allegiance was not home and so the flavour of life within it was never known because never loved. Whatever is said by a writer is, of necessity, said from within the small corner which he has occupied. Nothing can, with certainty, be said to apply to what happens elsewhere: it may be relevant to some extent or to no extent at all.

We who are appointed as the exponents of Christian faith in our own preserve, who speak or write in public places or more private ones, would probably be willing to acknowledge that we have not always had the vision which enables us to penetrate the contemporary debate and to lift it out of despond. We are bearers of good news, but our news is not always good enough. Perhaps it is sometimes too specifically religious and does not sufficiently embrace the disarrays of the world. Perhaps we forget or choose to ignore or have not yet been taught, in spite of St Paul, that man is of the earth, very earthy, and that it is at the level of his earthiness that lie the roots of his embryonic heavenliness.

When we speak of the meaning of man's unrest, do we succeed in proclaiming what God is doing through it, in spite of it, by means of it? When we speak of love, as we must and do, do we expect too much of those whom we address so that we berate their failure instead of showing love as the long-sought beginning of divine likeness which has to be striven for and suffered for and which is the final, latest, gift of grace heralding the dimension still to come? Do we say without uncertainty, when human pessimism asks what the world is coming to, that it is coming by a sure way to the kingdom of God?

Christianity has been itself in a land of two worlds, between the traditional certainties of the past and the new horizons of the present, between the accepted categories of the days gone by and the unexplored dynamics of the days we are now experiencing. We have far more effective tools than ever before in our knowledge of man's history and make-up with which to draw the picture of man's earthiness and of his coming heavenliness. We have the key with which to tell that the dramatic miracle of man comes to its peak in that love, spirit and likeness to God are forged, created, brought to birth, out of the lowly context of man's flesh, blood, pain, passion, in the embrace of the creative purpose of God.

This is the larger coinage for which the spirit of man asks in days of costly human experience. We possess words like 'redemption' and 'salvation' which have the meaning of creative results brought from discouraging events. Sometimes we hide behind them and use them as shields for our uncertainties because we do not know how to explain the truths they conceal or to penetrate with that meaning into the arena of public unrest or of private suffering. Perhaps it is that in the true meaning of the word we do not prophesy; and that is a dereliction of our calling, for where there is no vision, the people perish.

No doubt life has always been and always will be a baffling affair and an exacting one. No doubt in knowledge of the outcome the Creator is content that it should be so. Not without deep insight were thinkers of old inspired to say that man was made in the image of God; that human personality was to be gifted with the capacity to know, and to see and wrestle with things which transcend the world dimensions of existence and which would

carry man into the realm of the eternal and the divine. The forming of such personality takes its quality from the experience it is
forced to undertake and the search it is forced to do, not least
the searching for truth and for God, who purposely does not make
the perceiving of himself effortless or easy. It is formed even
more profoundly by the grace which God gives in our seeking
and which our nature often fiercely resists lest we feel we are
losing control of ourselves.

If it is true that human personality is to be the crowning product of this creation, then the world probably or indeed assuredly
cannot be other than it is with all its intensities of pain and of love
and goodness. Nothing but such a diverse ruggedness would
serve as the matrix in which human personality growing into
likeness of God and reaching out for possession of divine nature
could possibly be produced.

The forming of the physical world and of the whole universe
has been, so we believe, a process of upheaval and tension and
the clash of forces. What we are seeing and are ourselves involved
in is the process of creation still at work, no longer only at the
physical level but now most crucially at the level of mind, spirit
and relationship. There need be no surprises if this phase of
creation, not now in the making of inanimate rock, ocean or hill,
but of men and women striving towards their completion, is also,
and even more, turbulent and restless. A pain-free existence
might be capable of producing some kind of sentient being (Who
knows? There is no such thing as a pain-free existence!), but
it could surely not produce the kind of being whom God has
designed to be a sharer of his nature, his life and his creative
imagination. God also has travailed in pain in the accomplishment
of his creation and he has permitted us to know that love which
does not travail and suffer and overcome is not what love is
ultimately able to be.

Thus we come to the key which runs through this inquiry and
which can give Christianity a fresh perspective, strewn along its
way with new gifts of insight upon our condition and upon our

wonderings. Knowing now all that we know, Christianity can only be understandable in terms of the all-inclusive process of which evolution tells. In it we have a glimpse of the comprehensiveness of divine purpose in which all the dis-array and unrest, the freedom and the evil, the intimations of love and beauty, are swept in to the creative process. The prophets of science have enabled the exponents of religion to prophesy again.

✑ 3 ❧

Good News Not Good Enough

NEW THINGS HAVE, throughout Christian history, emerged
from the general realm of scientific discovery to shake the existing
patterns of Christian belief, and every time this has happened
Christianity has ended up strengthened, deepened and enlarged.
There is no strong wind of truth which can blow this house down
because new truth can only add to truth and deepen the foundation on which belief rests. The reality which the Christian
religion strives to describe can suffer nothing but enrichment
from the reality into which the scientists are probing. Strong
winds have been blowing in all parts of Christendom, and
where these have been greeted with fearless flexibility and with
trust in God's handling of the emerging creation, only good has
come.

In the particular direction of evolution, and in what evolution
has to say about the origin of man, it has become unmistakably
clear that Christianity must once again undergo a stretching of its
arteries and acceptance of some new horizons of thought. The
simple fact of man's long development from humble origins, as
compared with his ready-made manufacture at the hand of God,
has profound consequences.

The truths embedded in these stories concerning man's
characteristic temptations and his reactions to the awareness of
guilt will never grow dim or even be unworthy of study. But
nobody in the Western world any longer feels obliged to
accept that here is an authoritative statement of the way in which
the world, its flora, fauna and human occupants came into
being.

All races have their mythological and semi-religious stories about man's origin. They may seem fanciful to the modern mind, but they arose from observation of the human scene and represent the attempt to get at the root of the whys and wherefores of life's mysteriousnesses. The accounts of creation in the book of Genesis are part of a body of folklore which was common to the Jews and to the surrounding people of the ancient Middle East. They were stories of a mythological kind like any others, but in the hands of the chosen people and under the influences of Judaism, they were moulded into a more specifically moral and religious shape. They were designed to tell something significant about the relation between God and man and would not have claimed to be in our sense factual or scientific. Geology, archaeology and anthropology were not yet on the scene.

What these myth-stories tell us is that man was created in a ready-made perfection 'in the image and likeness of God' in the Garden of Eden. Because of the supposed innocent perfection of those first representatives of the human race, it had to follow that the far-from-innocent imperfections of their descendants had to be accounted for. The answer which seers of old arrived at as the only possible explanation was that, at some very early time after the creation, those distant ancestors of the human race – in the persons of Adam and Eve – underwent a catastrophic fall from that supposed moral innocence and that this had brought in its train all the ills of man and all the imperfections of the world order. Sin, pain, enmity, hatred, disease, death were all lumped together as having stemmed from the fall.

Like those of old, Christian thinkers found no alternative way of diagnosing the causes of human disarray, and so for the whole span of Christian history these beliefs have continued to hold the field. And it all fitted in very well. The Christian revelation came in fulfilment of Old Testament expectations. The Genesis story was of fallen perfection, love gone wrong, divine likeness in man defaced, obedience become rebellion. So therefore in continuity with the Old Testament beginnings Christianity had to say that the coming of Christ and particularly the suffering of Christ brought the reversal of this catastrophe: man's sin forgiven, love renewed, the divine likeness restored, man given a fresh start, God's honour satisfied.

Christian thinkers from St Paul onward hammered out within these terms of reference a splendid orthodoxy which has illuminated Christendom and the world ever since. From the Epistle to the Romans onwards this became the classic doctrine underlying what theologians call the theory of atonement. That is the set of ideas which tells how it is that Christ's offering of himself to crucifixion and death undid the damage caused by the original fall and the continuing sin of mankind. It is among the largest of the problems in Christianity, if not the largest of all. On its central questions of precisely how the suffering of Christ accomplished these 'inestimable benefits' for mankind, and of what took place in that cataclysmic event towards God, towards man and in relation to the powers of evil, Christian theorizing will doubtless never cease. In its history it has gone round in puzzled and sometimes devious circles, seeking answers to what seem like unfathomable questions.

Nevertheless, that orthodoxy has served the Christian generations as was providentially intended. It is a system of belief hallowed by the ages, supported by scripture, confirmed by Christian experience. To it untold numbers of people owe their coming to a relationship with God through Christ. But it is a system which inevitably bears the marks of an earlier age and there are, it may be guessed, other untold numbers who may owe their rejection of Christianity and their impatience with Christian teaching to the seeming obscurantism of a system which holds on to an out-of-date idea of the world and to a belief which pins upon man the guilt of all the world's non-perfection.

That might in truth not matter, for Christianity does not trim its sails in order to please man or to satisfy his intellect. It is permitted to be a rock of offence and a stone of stumbling, and it is for man to yield to God's truth, not for God's truth to yield to man.

But that is not to say that Christianity is absolved from being open to new thought nor that it is permitted to ignore the tide of knowledge flowing in the world. The promise is that the church will be led into all truth. Sometimes new knowledge must be absorbed and digested even though it may seem at first to be of a somewhat alien or unwholesome kind. It will invariably turn out that it is wholly nourishing and that it underwrites Christianity's integrity.

Christianity eventually accepted the astronomy of Copernicus and Galileo and thus came to terms with a whole new range of understanding about the creative activity of God. It must now do the same down to the last implications of the more terrestrial discoveries of Darwin and his followers. Here again there is a great new area of Christian exploration to be undertaken which will deepen understanding about man and God, about suffering and about the coming of Christ.

It is not to be wondered at that these questions revolving round the fall of man, the disarray of the world and the suffering of Christ have been baffling to the Christian mind since, as it now appears, the impossible attempt was being made to match an historical fact (in the coming of Christ) with a mythological surmise (in the fall of man). No doubt the understanding of Christ will never cease to grow, but at least it can now be taken a large step further through our new understanding of man, the creature of evolution.

If we now allow ourselves to regard man as a creature formed gradually and painfully over aeons of evolutionary process, new vistas of possible clarification immediately begin to appear over the horizon. But it is necessary to abandon every kind of backward-looking belief in original innocence. All the deeper levels of spiritual insight concerning God as Creator of the moral texture of the universe are to be retained unaltered, but perfection and fall at the outset of man's career on earth must be set aside as legendary idealism. From this also there will follow the abandonment of that equally backward-looking idea of the lost faithfulness of past generations and the rather favourite preaching point of returning to erstwhile Christian standards and spiritual values – as though our ancestors were some kind of paragons. Distance may not altogether make the heart fonder but it gives the mind a refuge in which to hide from the realities of the present.

The question for Christianity is whether this new step can be taken while retaining all that is essential to that splendid orthodoxy. The answer is that it can. The orthodoxy is not destroyed but confirmed.

The question for the ordinary thinking person is whether this new perspective throws more light on the meaning of life on earth and of its frequent painfulness. The answer is that it does. The painfulness is shown as a necessity of the divine scheme and as the underside of the love which awaits its final completion in each person.

It is now certain that the human race had its beginning far down the biological ladder in the primal life-forms from which the whole animal kingdom arose. Man in fact was not born in some kind of innocent perfection but in the mud of some primaeval lagoon. Even were there scientifically any residual doubts about this (and there seem not to be), it would still strike us as being the more likely explanation, since we can observe that nothing of any sort whatever comes into this world ready made. The whole creative procedure appears to be based on growth and development – on growing and becoming – and even Christ had no dispensation from womb and birth and from the rigours of growth into manhood. Moreover, even in spirit his perfection had to be reached through the things he experienced and suffered.

Of the fact of evolutionary origin as compared with instant creation there is no reasonable doubt, even though there may still be debates about the means and mechanisms by which evolution operates. For our purpose it is the fact of evolution which matters; the simple thesis that man had his origin at the bottom of the ladder among primitive forebears shared alike by animal and man. But now there comes one of those paradoxes which are met with frequently in the discussion of spiritual matters and which arise from the fact that man's nature is not in a single dimension but in a double one. Fortunately we are not concerned with the technical aspects of the matter from a biological point of view. Work still proceeds on heredity and its related cytology, transmission of characteristics, the place of enzymes in survival technique and other subjects.

Man is an evolutionary creature, carrying with him all the accumulated equipments and powers which stamp him as having come from the animal kingdom and which have enabled him to reach a pinnacle position in it. But at the same time he is a crea-ture – he alone among all other living creatures – of the threshold of love, and evolution alone can no longer carry him to his des-tination. This is man's dramatic and often traumatic situation. He stands with evolution behind him and with the dimension of spirit or divinity or life eternal (it does not matter what name we use) before him, and the characteristic of this dimension is love. In essence he already belongs in part to that dimension and (often unbeknownst to himself) hankers for its realization.

Evolution does not therefore supply an answer to man's emergence from the exactions of life as though it were possible to say that, given time, mankind will evolve towards greater goodness and towards freedom from suffering (though there are those who say this and believe it). It does, however, offer us a particularly valuable clue to our understanding of the painfulness and seeming imperfection of life and of the way in which the divine scheme is at work. It is a clue upon which we almost cer-tainly could not have put our finger without the idea of evolution, and to which the old scheme of thinking did not admit us. It is no bigger maybe than a mustard seed, but it yields a trail of illumina-tion.

Looking back down the long corridor of our evolutionary
past now opened up, we see the powers and equipments with
which the human race has gradually been furnished. Accompany-
ing these, intimately connected with all of them, occupying
almost the entire centre of all our reactions, is pain. The whole
creation has been made vulnerable to pain, not as a moral consequence of sin but as a plain biological fact of life. Pain in all
probability stretches back to the most original and primitive stages
of life. Strange and surprising it may be, but here in the seemingly
dark fact of pain lies the catalyst of the moral task of man: the
catalyst which splits up the whole moral problem into its component parts.

Clergymen, the official exponents of Christianity (and the writer
of this book is one), have not had the ability to lift this area of
debate concerning the meaning of man's unrest. We are bearers of
good news, yet our news is seldom good enough. In spite of the
thinking and debating we do not speak with an assured voice
about what God is doing through that unrest, in spite of it and by
means of it. We make a show of exhortation or else we simply
moralize about sin, but we do not often enough tell this truth that
God works not only by means of sunshine but by means of storm
and darkness, transmuting these rough elements into agencies of
creation and kindlers of love. We are almost facile prophets who
talk as though a strong faith and a deep understanding, love and
goodness, were the expected norm in human and social relationships; and, when clearly they are not, we are apt to fall back on a
disapproving condemnation of society and on the formula of man's
sinfulness. We forget or choose to ignore or have not yet been
taught man's earthiness, and that it is at the level of earthiness that
we must first of all come to understand the reality of his make-up
and the substance of his motive. We must look for signs of right
and righteousness at a very earthy level and not in the manifest
spirituality of the proficient, and not find sin and apostasy in everything he does. Now the advent of evolution has brought us a

salutary reminder of what St Paul said, although he knew nothing
of evolutionary theory.

Only when we have grasped the picture of creation in a long,
slow advance from embryonic beginnings will the ground have
been prepared to make the exploration into the dramatic character of what we mean by spiritual destiny. We were not created
ready-made nor born in innocent perfection endowed with love
and spiritual quality. Our ancestry was in dust and water, to become after prodigious ages a creature of complete thought and
feeling. Our task is to explore how this human constitution,
backed by this humble ancestry and structured of vulnerable
flesh and blood (still now nourished exclusively from the earth as
reminder of our basic earthiness), is the complex in which is
destined to be formed spiritual man, man in the divine image, man
at the threshold of a participation in the life of God.

That trail of illumination begins at the fact that pain was companion to the very earliest biological ventures into life (deep in the
instincts of survival which made evolution possible), and it runs
onwards right through to man's own venture into freedom and
spiritual endeavour to a point of focus in Christ's sufferings and
on into our own unrest and disarrays and strivings. On the way it
casts its light on the causes of sin, on hidden levels of motive, on
the means by which evil plays on those motives to increase its
hold on man's conduct, and thence, arising from the consequences
of Christ's coming, on the inner structure of forgiveness, on the
overcoming and defeat of evil and on man's sanctification and
entry into the experiencing of dimensions of love properly termed
divine.

Strange and mysterious though it may seem, pain affords the
one single and most potent thread of continuity between earthiness and the spirituality of the human person. It is indeed the
thread on which the entire coherence of the creative intent of God
is to be (in the world) most fully understood. Refuse to coun-
tenance it and there is lost the principal key to the puzzle of
existence and the principal passport to spiritual progress. More

paradoxical still, there is lost the weapon by which the increasing advance of unrest is stayed. The meeting of pain is the heart of the strategy for the conquest of pain.

Nor is this any gloomy or miserable kind of pessimism if we look at the grand strategy of the purpose of creation. If pain was a powerful factor in evolutionary advance, it turns out that it is a factor fully as vital in man's progress to his eventual destiny and to the ultimate dimension of his being. No one could have preferred to have remained at the stage of our ancestral beginnings with no hope of attaining to the status of *homo sapiens*. In like token none who have glimpsed the intimations given in Christian belief of what awaits the finishing of creation would be likely to prefer extinction on this side of the threshold of love with no hope of attaining the fulfilment of so many half-perceived desires. To this sweep of continuity and to the curious significance in the divine providence of pain – ancient companion, protector and destroyer, friend and enemy, corrupter and refiner – evolution has been an open sesame.

Against this background we now see love slowly dawning, a new-comer amid the tougher ingredients of the evolutionary scene. It was not provided ready-made as part of the perfection reigning in Eden, as once we supposed. It kindled and struggled to existence when pain had long been indigenous to life. Over vast stretches of biological time love was still something for the future. The humbler ingredients of biological need (powered by thrust and urge and pain) drove the enterprise of evolution.

Love thus took its character from the need to stand against pain, bearing it for the protection of offspring, challenging its power to scare, confronting it and refusing to be deterred by it. This in increasing measure has been its character ever since. This is the character which came to its highest point in Christ. It had to strengthen its hold on motive and will, challenging barriers of reluctance and doing things of which evolution's logic must disapprove, like championing the weak and declining to retaliate.

At length when it came to its high point in Christ it was clean contrary to the principles of evolutionary urge, bidding man to lay down his aggression and open up his defences and show love's power by the very fact of its will to hold on in face of pain.

❧ 4 ❧

Things Old and New

THE HORIZONS OF our thinking about mankind have been greatly enlarged by the results of scientific discovery. We know very much more about ourselves than we once did and much more about our environment in the universe.

Cosmology and astro-physics have opened our minds to new truth about the prodigious size of the universe and about the relatively unimportant place which our solar system occupies. Intriguing problems of its origin and of its possible ending are being continuously more deeply penetrated. Geophysics has pieced together the movements which have brought our planet to its present shape and texture as a place where flora, fauna and humanity can exist. Biology and anthropology have unveiled much of the astonishing journey on which humanity (besides other species) has travelled from its primitive beginnings in the lower animal world to the complexity and competence of *homo sapiens*. Looking inwards upon man, psychology has explored the structures of personality in depth and has begun to understand some of its intricacies in their potentialities for health or disease.

At the centre of all this knowledge is man (and despite some enlightened questioning of man's central importance it is still the only valid estimate of his place in creation). New knowledge about the influence which produced and structured him cannot but deepen our understanding of him. We look at ourselves with a new realism. And that also means that we must look again at our ideas of God, because God reveals himself in his creation and most specially in the drama of humanity. Altogether we have gained from science a powerful sense of a creation in dynamic process. We have been given a wider understanding of what God is doing and how (and even perhaps why) he is doing it.

Evolution – the principle of that astonishing journey of all the species – is perhaps the most important key of all to our understanding of the creative purpose and of ourselves within it. It tells us (at the very least) that we have a far larger and more dramatic story behind us than used to be imagined in days not so very long ago when English Bibles had marginal notes added giving 4004 BC as the date of the creation. Now we know that at the back of us there is a great sweep of biological history, full of struggle and achievement as well as of pain and violence. It is impossible to suppose that these tremendous facts can be placed on one side of the balance without at the same time making a radical re-assessment of what lies on the other. New physical science calls for new spiritual science, and we have to make a ruthless and impartial examination of the weights on religion's side of the balance. Christianity stands by its concern with fact and truth, not by theory and surmise. Seek where we may, we shall find no historical or biological Eden nor any of that original perfection or moral innocence of which Eden legends are picture stories: no moral innocence, no spiritual awareness, no remotest concept of God, no sign as yet of love. Whether we look at man in his racial development or at a child in his growing from infancy to adulthood, the same principle holds and the same story is told of a beginning from which moral perfection and even moral awareness are absent; in which love in its early stages is dictated by biological need and only comes much later, after an apprenticeship in discipline and some striving, to be love of a more deep and authentic kind.

A state of either perfection or of moral innocence is too far away from what we now know of the distant history of man to be an acceptable basis for a whole theory of man's relation with God and of God's activity towards man.

A fall from innocence and a broken perfection provide too fragile an explanation for the massive turbulence and disarrays of the world – for not all turbulence is the result of wickedness nor all painfulness the consequence of sin. They are indeed more often than not the spur to progress and the stimulus of refinement.

A restoration of righteousness and a return to a perfection that once was is not of sufficiently deep dynamic to be the cause for which the incarnation of the Word of God took place. The perfection which lies at the end of the creative process is bound to be of more facets and of richer depth than an initial perfection which had not suffered the rigours of the process. We are to see that it was in the forging of such an ultimate consummation that the Christ was engaged. The momentum of the journey of creation carries the mind forward in the quest for perfection and not in any respect backwards.

If we do look backwards, what we are to see is no perfection but the long earthy logic of evolutionary development which throws much more light on the phenomenon of man: a constitution of instinct, will and purpose of great depth and tenacity with which millennia of evolution have endowed our race. These in turn we can understand to be served by a great array of needs, desires, pains, vulnerabilities and fears which long experience of evolutionary struggle has laid down in the foundations of our consciousness. We see a tough competitive, aggressive and defensive mentality – in providential readiness for the divine alchemy.

This is the material – not the relics of a tattered perfection – out of which we are going to make sense of the great and enduring vision of Christian destiny.

Here is the basic reality of the double human possibility. These things provide the points at which evil intrudes and these same things are the points from which the final possession of spirit is built up. They are a battleground in which the most portentous issues are to be decided. First in Christ and thence in man, good and evil, life and death, light and darkness are the possibilities lying in reach of our evolutionary desires and vulnerabilities.

We are more than we thought of the earth, and our earthiness
is basically neutral, a raw material for moral and spiritual outcome. But that is not yet: we have not yet embarked on the
discussion about evil, not yet seen the implications of the freedom
in which the creature purpose has set us. We are still looking at
the argument that evolution gives us the only realistic basis for a
proper Christian discussion.

What we are going to see (when we reach that point in the
argument) is that the Christian revelation unfolds against the
background of this toughness and ruggedness and that it makes
sense only in view of it. Christianity has made the lasting contribution to religious thought that our quest for God must be made
in grateful recognition of our humanity and acceptance of the
world around us, not by an escape from and a rejection of them.
To this contribution is now added a whole new range of knowledge about the true make-up of this humanity of ours.

More important still, Christianity can tell that these very things
which sometimes we so much deplore – the competitiveness, the
vulnerability, the aggression and so forth – are the factors out of
which the supernatural dimension of our kinship with God is to be
forged. This, we shall see, is a significant part of what Christ was
doing for us in this arena of our freedom, this *milieu* of our quest
for love and for God. He was taking the powerful raw materials
which evolution has given us, which carry at the heart of them
the promise of a still unknown dynamic, and declaring the reality
of that dynamic when the supremacy of love has been finally
gained.

It is here at the full tide of what evolution has accomplished in
the forming of man that we perceive Christianity to have its
logical place in what God is doing in this world (for we do not
know much of what he is doing elsewhere in the creation). And
it is not any longer the process of evolution which is capable of
bringing the divine scheme to its appointed conclusion. It is not
evolution, nor human ingenuity, but a new creative action of
God which can mould these materials into their desired shape.

Evolution made the provision, but the divine love alone is capable of kindling the spirit and imparting the love which brings kinship with God.

Not a broken harmony from the past but one to be forged for the future; not an erstwhile love now desecrated but a love being challenged into existence by God's grace in man's nature. Moreover, if that nature is made of rugged and explosive materials (and it certainly is), we are going to discover by the same token that the love which challenges it is far from being the mild and sentimental article which opponents of Christianity have sometimes represented it to be. It is not mildness which is the secret cause of opposition for most people but the stringency and the exactingness of what love demands. We are going to see that only these evolutionary raw materials, powerful and explosive, and the divine strength of love, challenging and exacting, would be capable of producing the durable quality of what God desires for a coming kingdom.

All this will emerge in due time; and it follows from a recognition of the complex depths of our evolutionary human nature. Scientific discovery has forced us into a deepening of religious insight. There is a decisive difference between the Genesis picture of the origin of man and that of man risen from the long journey of evolution. In the light of it we shall be able to take an optimistic view of the world's unrest. Instead of nostalgia for a smooth passage in a calm ocean – hints of a lost perfection – we shall perhaps catch the picture of the hammering out through the thick and thin of human events, passions and relationships, of the long battle for the supremacy of love. In this we may already see the beginnings of a unity behind the scheme of things: the creation, the animal kingdom, the evolution of man, the dawn of love, the rise of religion, the coming of Christ, the revelation of a dimension of being after death.

Almost all Christian estimates of Genesis have undergone a tremendous change since the biblical scholarship of the last century disentangled the historical from the mythological sources of the early books of the Old Testament. It has been widely accepted that although full of inspired spiritual insight, the accounts of creation in these books do not represent – or even claim to represent – what we now call scientific or historical fact. There has been no difficulty in making an intelligent re-interpretation of the six days of creation and in seeing behind them to the majestic panorama of thousands of millions of years of geological preparation. However, as may be expected, the creation of man and particularly man's moral relationship with God is a very much more delicate matter. Tamper with that and the whole of religion is placed at risk. Call in question the fall of man and the whole structure of our beliefs about Christ is liable to collapse. So say some exponents of orthodox belief, and so it is that Christianity has not yet embarked on any profound re-appraisal of the framework it has traditionally known – creation, fall, condemnation of man, reversal of these by Christ's sacrifice, mankind's forgiveness and reconciliation with God. (Indeed this present writer finds himself looking over his shoulder for those who will be waiting to pounce on him at the slightest hint that he is falling into a heresy of this kind himself by tampering with the traditional structure!)

Nevertheless no heresy follows. The winds of scientific truth will not blow this house down. Christianity awaits a fresh assurance that there is in the divine scheme a positive and creative meaning – and not simply a doleful one concerning our wickedness – to all our pains and disarrays. If we can grasp this positiveness and also recognize that our wickedness is far from negligible, something will have been achieved. Our vision of divine strategy and the meaning of divine love will have been enhanced.

The proposition of mankind's evolutionary origin has enabled us to realize more of that earthiness on which Christianity, because of the incarnation, has tried (even if not always successfully) to have its thinking. Man's origin in the animal world and his possession still of many traits of character connecting him with that phase of his existence opens new doors and lets in a new light on his far from tamed nature.

This earthiness, or perhaps better this down-to-earthiness, is the setting of the stage for the extraordinary and dramatic position in which man is placed. Alone among all that has been created, we, men and women, must make the transition from the earth-born to the heaven-born. We, creatures of evolution, are not permitted to be content with what evolution has given us. We, uniquely, are destined for a dimension of being beyond all that earth and evolution can do or even wish to contend with. There lies before us, evolutionary creatures that we are in so much of our origin and instinct, the exacting destiny of entry into the *milieu* of divinity. There is already set in our heart a certain unclear yet very compelling hankering for something beyond ourselves. We are inspired and also plagued by intimations of our potential immortality! The hankering which compels us at one level clashes with the earthen hankerings in our evolutionary make-up which drives us at other levels. Belonging no longer to the animal kingdom, we are divided between the pull of our spiritual destiny and the pull of our evolutionary nature.

This is the meaning of much of our unrest: a travail unknown to any of our erstwhile companions in creation. Out of the lowliness of flesh and instinct and desire – all the things which nature and evolution have given us – we alone must contend with the aspiration to be higher than angels, participants in the divine nature of God. It is not possible to suppose that the whole created universe exists for this purpose and is organized round this happening. Even if the same thing is taking place in other planets and in other galaxies beyond our own (as well it may be), the same dramatic quality is likely to attach to it the agonizing metamorphosis from lowliness of flesh and blood to glory of spirit and love.

The characteristics which distinguish us humans here are almost bound to be similar in other beings elsewhere, if they exist at all. God is God and God's love is God's love for everywhere: he does not change. Human personality is capable of knowing and of expressing that which is divine. Of this the decisive fact is that God in Christ adopted human personality not as a temporary expedient but as a permanent expression of his divinity. Humanity therefore, as we know it and possess it, must be the *milieu*, wherever it may be, in which kinship with the divine is by divine grace fostered.

There are in the creation spiritual beings of different kinds, angels and archangels, spiritual powers of evil and darkness, cherubim and seraphim. And there are (in this world at least) animal creatures of vastly varying kinds. In the middle as it were there is man; and only man and only Christ with man undergo the life-and-death travail of entry to the dimension of spirit and of love. Only the company of heaven know the gulf that lies between humanness and what religion calls redemption, and only they have travailed in passing from one to the other. If there are beings, as some surmise, of superlative skill – little green men or the occupants of flying saucers – they may be spiritual beings as angels are, but they are not then humans destined for participation in divine nature. Only those who share the common flesh and blood which Christ also shared are destined to share the divinity which he came to bestow on his fellow sons of God. In the terms which we are here using, only the creatures of evolution are destined for the divine kinship which lies outside evolution, beyond the threshold of the entry into love.

Life has been continuously challenged to explore and come to terms with new regions either of physical environment or, later, of psychic experience. It would be for the biologist to tell of the various ventures on which life has embarked in its onward progress. One at least can be named as decisive, which was when life first dragged itself from the marine surroundings of its origin to the alien and hazardous environment of dry land. Teilhard de Chardin has suggested that this, and all the other major barriers which life has negotiated, was accompanied by a great expenditure of effort and thus a certain experience of pain. The amateur in these matters might moot the idea that another crucial stage – spread over a long period – was the early dawning of consciousness, herald of so much to come if not of everything to come.

For our purposes here in sketching the broad sweep of events it is only useful to highlight two points of reference. From earliest and most primitive beginnings life eventually came to the first crucial threshold which evolution has presented. This was when rational self-consciousness began to distinguish protoman from his predecessors and he drew at long last decisively away from the animal kingdom and became truly man. The first threshold introduced man to humanness and to the dawn of spiritual awareness. The second and more crucial threshold is that to which his humanness, his awareness of spirit and his strengthening of moral consciousness soon brought him. That is where man now stands, painfully and slowly learning a new language and exploring a new environment, no longer an evolutionary language or a biological environment but a language of spiritual perception and an environment of supernatural struggle and exploration. That is the threshold of love: the threshold beyond which love's supremacy – glimpsed but still unknown – awaits a full establishment and a full experience.

It is as an integral part of this great sweep of events that in due time there took place the incarnation. The coming of Christ brought man to the central arena of the threshold and the challenge of love. It cannot be without significance, nor is it simply a pious fancifulness that Christianity has insisted all the way through that Christ's divinity (of which the virgin birth is the indication), as well as his humanity, is real. Here, in the terms we are using, is the man who is at one and the same time the man born from within evolution and the man begotten of the creative fountainhead outside it, fountainhead whose quality is love. He came experiencing, creating and exploring in this arena of man's free-

dom; as man, experiencing life, and as Word of God creating out
of that experience an ultimate supremacy of love; as man sharing
mortality, and as Word of God forging mortality into the means
of immortality. When mankind had become sufficiently ready to
face the reality of the threshold of love, the Christ came (as an
integral part of the creative process) to hammer out the principles
of man's transition over this astonishing divide and to shepherd
him through the exacting transformation from his earthiness to
his ultimate heavenliness. He alone among mankind passed
totally over the threshold, having brought the entire legacy of
evolution finally under the supremacy of love for the purpose of
eternal life, promising that we too, in consequence of his passing,
might be enabled to do the same.

What we have to understand about Christ's suffering (in
addition to understanding it as confrontation with evil and dealing with sin) is that he was with full intent laying himself open to
the point where all the human vulnerabilities inherited from
evolution converge. He carried in himself the entire legacy of
evolution: physical mortality, vulnerability to pain, knowledge of
fear, the prospect of the end of consciousness and the deprivation
of being. He came thus to the inevitable conclusion of all that
evolution can offer to the individual. He met the dissolution which
lies inescapably at the heart of evolutionary heritage – and consequently at the heart of every man and woman. At this most
inward (and terrifying) point he gave to evolution another conclusion and to the individual a new vista of immortality. He made
the evolutionary heritage the vehicle of a new kind of life. The
gates of hell will not prevail; the human soul will not see corruption; the keys will open the doors of the kingdom. Christ, the
man of evolution, stood (and still stands) at the precise point
where death takes over. There Christ the Word of God translates
the fact of death and the experience of death into the fact of new
life and the experience of resurrection.

Further, we are going to find that this very process of forging the linkway from past to future contains within itself the

'mechanism' by which also evil is confronted and sin is prevailed over and forgiven. It is necessary to point out very clearly that there is no such thing for us humans as a purely spiritual level and that the spirit and the body are never mutually exclusive. What happens in the spirit happens through the medium of our bodily fabric – flesh, nerve, brain, emotion, pain, will and all the rest. Spirit is rooted at the deepest level of humanness. This is of the utmost importance for the understanding of ourselves and for the yielding of all our experiences to the creative purpose of God. It is of the utmost importance equally in realizing that the prodigious creative act in Christ had, of necessity, to be accomplished through the medium of flesh, nerve, brain, emotion, pain, will and all the rest.

Evil obtains its purpose through the dreads and painfulnesses as well as through the desires of evolutionary nature. Sin exists where evil deflects (by dread or desire) the will from a way which would be nearer to that of love. In meeting the legacies of evolution at the points of greater vulnerability Christ was transforming the vulnerabilities, and all evolution with them, into the elements of eternity and spirit, contending with evil's bid to deflect his will away from the way of love – exactly what happens in temptation to you and me. He was refusing to let dread (of pain) or desire (for escape from it) lead him into sin. The open meeting with vulnerability was opening the way to the supremacy of love over all aspects of human personality.

God the Creator provided the evolutionary fabric of man's being just as surely as he also gave the coming of Christ and the gifts of the spirit. It was to be, with all its vulnerabilities, exactly the *milieu* in which spirit, love and kinship with the divine could be forged, nurtured and established.

So much for the long sweep and the broad canvas. For the purpose of this discussion it has been necessary first and foremost to establish the fact that man actually is a creature of evolution and that he really did reach the status of manhood through the path-

ways of evolutionary advance. Upon the certainty of this the
biologist would no doubt insist; and, as we have seen, there are
persuasive reasons from the religious angle that such is the truth
of the matter. When we come to man, the individual, we must
find those characteristics which, belonging to him and to Christ,
are most particularly the ingredients and raw materials of man's
spiritual exploration and of Christ's consummation of it. What in
evolution are the things which play the profoundest and most
prominent parts in man's conduct towards his fellow and towards
his Creator?

Most of the instincts with which we shall be concerned are
those which represent the biological equipment for survival and
for that natural selection and adaptation of which evolution
consists. They are the equipments of the animal kingdom, though
in man deepened, strengthened, more subtle, sometimes more
refined, sometimes more demonic. They consist of the natural
urges safeguarding the necessities of living – the requirements of
food, space, warmth, freedom from damage, freedom to procreate.
These are put into practice by a natural competitiveness – running
through all our activities – which can be diagnosed under the
heading of self-defence and aggression. Beneath these lie the
more basic instincts of the desire to live and enjoy; and the dread
of pain and of annihilation. And of these two, perhaps surprisingly,
we are going to discover that the dread of pain is more powerful
than the desire to enjoy. We have, then, pain and pleasure, the
dreads and desires which are linked to them, and thence the defence and aggressions which secure them. What we are going to
do as we proceed is to work out what the arrival of love into the
human scene did to these things and how (following the pioneering of Christ in this region) they are taken from the control of evil
into which they easily fall and are swept into the service of creation, as the only raw material there is of spiritual personality. That,
again, is the drama of the human situation. No want is saved, no
sudden perfection given. It is not that we humans have souls that
are immortal; we have something far more dramatic, which is

souls that are capable of being raised to immortality. Our ultimate spiritual status is created out of absolute lowliness of origin;
created from a never-ceasing struggle to lay hold of love and thus
of kinship with God through the medium of our bodies and senses.
We are creatures who, as a race in the long sweep of history and as
individuals in the shorter personal term, have started from the
bottom. Our divine image and our kinship with divine nature are
forged out of the responses and the disciplines, the pains and the
desires of all those evolutionary equipments which make us, each
one of us, the creatures that we are. And it is not evolution which
does the creating and the spiritual forging, but God. More
specifically it is Christ, the man of evolution, Son of Man, the man
of the divine dimension, Word of God, who by means of struggle,
pain, desire and faith became in himself the final product of the
creative intention.

If we do not from now on see Christ exactly as the inherited
ideas have portrayed as coming to *reverse* the consequences of the
fall and to *restore* to man the shattered image and the forfeited
favour of God, we can begin to see something more contemporary
and more practical. We see him, himself the owner of a frame of
evolutionary instinct and human frailty, embracing the pain and
disarray of it all and forging from it the final shape of humanity
and the final kinship with God.

If we need any further indication of orthodoxy it is to be seen
in that at the heart of this embracing of painfulness we are to
discover the bedrock meaning of forgiveness. The whole argument from evolution brings us irrevocably to that central Christian
point of forgiveness: God's love to us and ours to one another.
There we shall also find the beginning of the defeat of evil.

The love which remains unchanged in face of pain – the love
that will not let me go, that will not make reprisal, that does not
desire to condemn – is the central heartland of the meaning of
forgiveness. For that there is need ever and again as much between person and person as between God and the individual soul.
To support the authenticity of this we do not need any kind of

doctrine of the wholesale damning of mankind drawn from long
pre-Christian thinking. We need only the evidence of everyday
life and, whether known or not in any particular individual experience, the alchemy of which forgiveness is the secret.

❧ 5 ❧

The Damning of Man

IN DAYS NOT long past, a simple little sentence was sometimes used in school to demonstrate the value of clear thinking in the abstract. It was this: 'a negro is a man with woolly hair, but a man with woolly hair is not necessarily a negro.' This could be transposed to the region of our inquiry here if one were to say: 'Man's wickedness causes much grief and suffering, but grief and suffering are not necessarily caused by man's wickedness.' Christianity has been hard put to it to make distinctions of this kind and has been unable to give an assessment of the turbulences and unrests of the world that bear a sense of purpose, meaning or constructiveness. It has been easier to take a line of least resistance and to place the blame for all imperfections on the wickedness of man. It is all too true that 'the evil that men do lives after them', and that it fans out to touch and hurt more people than were involved in the original evil act or intention. But it is also true that there is a whole range of griefs and sufferings, turbulences and unrests which are in a sense morally neutral and are indigenous to the creative process. The dilemma in which Christianity has found itself in making this distinction and consequently in being able to speak with a constructive, positive voice about these things comes from a particular bit of belief which has been basic to the traditional view of things held by Christendom as a whole.

For the whole stretch of Christian history, and practically speaking up to this present day, there has been no alternative for Christian thinkers but to take as the base-line in their understanding of humanity the account of man's origin in the book of Genesis. The Genesis stories were the means by which men of old sought to account for the existence of evil and of pain in the creation. The creation had come from the hand of God and God had seen that it was good. How could there have come into this God-made perfection such alien, un-Godlike imperfections? It must have been through man's fault, for mankind was indeed seen to be frequently desperately wicked. Some cataclysmic moral disaster must have taken place through which man had fallen from his high estate of being in the image and likeness of God.

The story of man's perfection and fall is full of valuable spiritual insight and of remarkable psychological understanding. It will never cease to be useful in reminding a person of what happens to a human soul which finds itself having sinned and being in the grip of guilt. Nevertheless, as an account of what actually happened we now know that this certainly cannot be regarded as historical fact. Christianity, born out of that Jewish background, adopted as its own those parts of Judaism which had not been explicitly rejected by Christ – such as the less spiritual manifestations of the law as interpreted by Pharisaism. After all, Christianity itself had no other means of accounting for the world's troubles and sufferings than the ones which those Jewish thinkers of old had formulated. The idea of original perfection, of a pristine world of innocence which was shattered by a tragic moral disaster, became the unquestioned basis of the Christian view of man's relation with God and of the cause of Christ's coming. It was profoundly elaborated by St Paul and it made a theory of beautiful symmetry and neatness, as is exemplified in a sentence like, 'For as by one man's disobedience many were made sinners, so by one man's obedience many shall be made righteous' (Romans 5.19). From the Epistle to the Romans onwards this became the classic doctrine underlying what theologians call the problem of atonement, which aims to tell how it is that Christ's offering of himself undid and made right the damage and broken relationships caused by the fall of man. That problem has stretched the mind and vision of all the great thinkers and none has found a wholly satisfactory answer. Perhaps it will always be unfathomable to the mind of man. Yet little by little more light is shed and we are allowed more understanding. Is it possible and even remotely permissible to start tampering with a matter so large and so sacrosanct?

Answer how you will with horror or with agreement, it is now at this precise time unavoidable. A gap of credibility is open and Christian teaching has to try to present a false equation. Mankind did not come into this world ready made, for nothing ever does or has. Man was born in the dust and mud of primaeval seas and has struggled through millennia of evolution to reach manhood. Christ, the man of history whose religion is founded on fact and on action, cannot be understood in reference to a legendary and mythological account of mankind's condition. Son of man, he is himself man of evolution among men of evolution and must be understood as bringing the reality of the divine love to bear on the earthy mortal facts of the evolutionary situation.

There was no height from which to fall, no perfection to disrupt: all was originally primitive, all in a state of growing and of gradual evolutionary becoming. There was no relationship with the Creator to break, no ready-given morality to flout, no tested innocence to corrupt. Even the very capacities where these would come to consciousness were no more than in the long process of being formed. This is what the truth of evolution tells us, and wise men and wise women have wondered about it and many have written about it, to some extent. But the implications of this have not been faced nor the results of it assimilated into the life-blood of Christianity. To believe in the biological – and enthralling – fact of evolution is one thing: to see how it alters our view of what goes on around us is quite another. The difference between being created in ready-made perfection and having arisen in evolutionary hazard and competition over vast aeons of time is very considerable. It reveals some things which, discerned in the depths of our own make-up, can be understood as originating in the depths of our ancestry, back down that long corridor of our evolutionary development. It tells more about how man and woman succumb to evil than any legend of long ago can tell. And to the coming of Christ, while detracting nothing from the majestic scope of its meaning, it gives a wider significance than that of undoing the dawning of man.

The traditional Christian interpretation of the sufferings and unrests of man and of his world has been that they are the consequences, directly or indirectly, of man's fallen nature and undisciplined desires. The dilemma in which the idea of original perfection places Christianity is this: the blame for everything that appears to be in disarray in the creation must inevitably be laid on mankind, for it cannot after all be the fault of God. So the damning of man is logically insurmountable. Original sin and even total depravity are the ruling factors in man's condition. Original righteousness and the image of God are in sad tatters. Behind the image of what men and women are, Christian thought slips too easily into seeing what they might have been and perhaps once were and ought to be again. So, similarly, ordinary people look that way at the world, backwards to what was or what might have been. But what we must look to is not any kind of past perfection but to the ultimate perfection towards which this entire creative enterprise is heading.

If it is desired to demolish an existing argument or theory, it is no good spending time and energy picking holes in it. The thing to do is simply to put up a better argument. This whole book is an attempt to do exactly that about the meaning of man's unrest amid God's creative purpose. Yet Christianity's traditional positions are so entrenched, and so difficult to see round, that it is worth while looking at some of the anomalies in these foundations. Interestingly, that curious but valid phenomenon 'the spirit of the age' has begun to demand a deeper acknowledgment of human value, specially for the less privileged of this world. Its symptoms are to be seen in the nationalism of once-colonial peoples, in the battle for better wages, housing and working conditions, and in greatly sharpened sense of concern and compassion, not least on the part of young people, towards the homeless, the helpless and the otherwise socially deprived. People beg leave to wonder whether the religious account is the true account of the phenomenon of man. The willingness to consider human beings as carrying a burden of guilt and a degraded image of goodness has worn notably thinner: original sin never did seem to be a very just doctrine to some people. It is also interesting that while Christianity was busy laying the blame for the world's imperfections on the shoulders of man, the man in the street was busy questioning the goodness and even the existence of God, asking the question 'Why does God allow such things?' The church's condemnation of man was partly responsible for the world's condemnation of God.

But there are solider reasons than this for calling in question the erstwhile framework of Christian teaching on these matters.

First it implies that the Creator's plan was not really (for want of a better word) watertight – and this most of all in respect of the central purpose of his creation, man. If sin is so great an outrage to the Creator's love and if man is so radically damned for it, it cannot but seem that the perfection was intended to remain unsullied. This means that God made a miscalculation about the consequences of the freedom he has bestowed upon humanity. To be absurdly anthropomorphic, the Creator must have been disagreeably taken by surprise at this untoward turn of events. If, however, it was by divine permission, the condemnation cannot, justly, have been what it is supposed to be.

Secondly, it means that the incarnation of Christ was a special emergency measure forced upon the Father by the desperate plight of his creation. In order to put right what had gone wrong, Christ had to undergo a bloody and unjust death which should not have needed to happen. Had man not made a mess of things, Christ need not have become man to be crucified and killed. But this simply does not do as a description of the way in which the divine wisdom dealt with the creation.

The solidest reason of all for taking a fresh look is that Christ

himself does not seem to have theorized about perfection and fall
in the way in which St Paul and later theologians did. His attitude
was one which faced and accepted the turmoils and hazards, ups
and downs, of existence as being part and parcel of the field in
which God worked. He saw in the ruggedness of life the divine
purpose at work. He did not condemn the ruggedness and indeed
did not come to condemn at all. He came to take away things
which offend and are capable of turning man back from the
sources of divine life. If he was 'lifted up' to declare the supremacy
of love, he would draw all men to him. Because man is profoundly
vulnerable to evil and is ever and again goaded to doing evil
things and deterred from doing good things, the supremacy of
love declared by Christ is the meaning of forgiveness as needful
between man and man as between man and God.

As we pursue this inquiry with the facts of evolution rather
than the surmises of legend as our root position, there will
emerge the exhilarating prospect that the grandeur of man is
drawn out by just such a ruggedness as this and that amid the
hazards and pains and caprices of freedom his spiritual stature
moves towards its ultimate destination; for Christ too (so says the
Epistle to the Hebrews) was made perfect by suffering.

Besides this, the providential scheme in which God has made
his creation will appear as a self-consistent whole without changes
of mind or of plan or emergency measures; such things are
characteristic only of human indecision and imagination. The
coming of Christ will seem to be as indigenous to the divine plan
as the making of man, not prompted by any necessity that was not
in the divine mind before ever the world was.

✥ 6 ✥

A Death Before Life Was

A CLUE IN THE direction of such a comprehensive and integrated view of divine providence is offered to us in the book of Revelation. There, in two different places, the author speaks of the Christ as the Lamb as it had been slain before the foundation of the world. It is a tiny clue, but it is as though a corner of the curtain had been lifted to give a glimpse of the pre-cosmic divine economy. In it we are permitted to see God not in his all-powerfulness but in the moral aspect of his creatorship. What this tells us is that in the very intention to create, 'or ever the earth and the world were made', God foreknew the suffering that must accompany his purpose, and the sacrifice which its accomplishment must involve for himself. This is no glorious blueprint of perfection for a ready-made utopian creation. If there is suffering and sacrifice in prospect for the Creator, it can only be because the creation itself must groan in travail and because that travail must be part-shared, part-borne by the one who has fashioned it. By whom else might the Lamb have been slain but by the loved and desired creation itself? At what other hands should this seemingly astonishing enormity have been perpetrated but at the hands of the people whom the Creator has designed to be in his own likeness and who appear to find that destiny so hard? There is no glorious blueprint of instant perfection, but the glory of the ultimate outcome is not in doubt and the glory of the beginning is the moral glory of which we catch sight. It is that no prospect of travail or sacrifice would ever be such as might deter the divine love from setting out on the road of its achievement. There is a magnificently unconditional 'Come-what-may' heart in this intention, as there is in the marriage vow of 'for better for worse'. Indeed the marriage vow is explicitly stated to be a microcosm of the Christ-church, God-world, Creator-creation relationship and is intended to portray this very thing, that love is not deterred and that love which is deterred is not yet truly love. In the divine family conclave concerning the enterprise of creation (all our words have to be heavily anthropomorphic about these things), we see the Lamb, the Logos, the Word, the second person of the Trinity, the Christ-to-be, already in principle reconciled to the absolute necessity of sacrifice and thus to the absolute certainty of what will come in creation terms to be called sin. It is divine intent, reconciliation in principle, the willingness to pay the price of what will be. But there is a great gap between that and the practical fulfilment of the intention, between the will of the Divine Word and the suffering of the Christ in the human arena. In that gap are the limitless unknowns of every variation and caprice of event which freedom may bring forth, and the rising of the love-potential of the incarnate Christ to meet every possible occasion to which that freedom may give birth. Between the intention and the accomplishment there is the very subtle and very astonishing fact that the pre-existent Word must himself, in his Christhood, move forward into realized, in-hard-created-fact-achieved perfection. For even he, the captain of our salvation, was made perfect in sufferings. The hard-fact world is the phenomenon without which love could not come to its total expression, and without which, therefore, God could not enjoy the fullness of Godhead.

To build this much on what is admittedly a tiny clue may seem to be a castle in the air or a house built on the sand. The Revelation vision itself, let alone any spinning of interpretations from it, could be said to be only a transposing of the known facts of the incarnation and passion into the realm of pre-creation timelessness. It is true that the Christ was slain, but is anyone justified in claiming therefore that 'before time was' the Godhead was content in foreknowing that it must be so? It may be that it was, as has been said of old, a tragedy, an accident, a needless horror which would not have happened but for mankind's wickedness.

It is, however, not on the Revelation vision alone that this wholeness of divine intent with emergent fact is based. Revelation gives a clue, a clue leads to a discovery and discovery points towards an answer. I have indicated that the elements out of which we may surmise the divine plan had principally to be forged (or conversely the elements which we may unravel as factors of the divine plan) are growth, freedom, pain, evil, sin, forgiveness, love. It can be shown that all of these seemingly diverse elements dovetail elegantly (as the mathematician would put it) into one another in such a way that no one of them could exist without each and every one of the others. No love without sin, no humanity without freedom, no growth without pain, no freedom without evil, no forgiveness without love, no love without pain and as many more equations as there are combinations of words. I have said earlier that pain occupies a crucial and catalystic place in this whole analysis. It should and could be found in each of the equations. The role of pain will be analysed separately later on and its dominant position will be brought to light. For the moment the object is to show the interdependence of all the basic elements on each other. It is quite obvious why this is important. If evil and sin are indispensable factors in the creation, then the Christ was not called in to patch up a messy situation which had gone sadly wrong, nor was (and is) man the culprit at the centre of the 'mess'. Secondly, if pain is also indispensable, then it is possible to refute the popular misconception that pain is an alien intruder into what should otherwise be a comfortable world and that it is proof of the fact that things have 'gone wrong' or that God is not what we thought he was. Furthermore, if we can withdraw pain from being one of the symptoms of the messy situation, we shall at least be able to assess its true function and discover it in its true colours and depth of focus. The bracket which has conventionally held together 'pain and sin' as indicating the bad things in this world can also at last be deleted and the two erstwhile rogue partners can be placed in their true ecological relationship. Some writers have addressed themselves to the problem of how there can exist evil in a universe supposedly organized by love. In so doing they have taken for granted that pain is simply a part of evil and have thus lost the most important tool in disentangling the problem, which is the moral independence of pain.

The integral view of divine providence which can show it as embracing all diverse elements from the beginning until the end must begin from what little we know of mankind's destiny. In so far as our clouded vision can penetrate the matter, it can be said that the divine intention is to create a humanity that has all the potentiality of being drawn, through a conscious relationship with the Creator, into the possession of love and thus into participation in the divine nature of the Godhead. The fulfilment or realization of this potentiality results in mankind's gaining his goal of enjoying God for ever and in God's receiving his fulfilment in sharing his glory with a people thoroughly prepared for that eternal enjoyment. Since love comes into being as a response and cannot be commanded into existence, it must arise within a circumstance of freedom: indeed response presupposes freedom. Both response and freedom are phenomena attached to growth, for both science and religion would concur in saying that nothing springs ready-made or fully-formed into existence; if it did, it would neither be free nor be able to respond. The idea of growth is an irreducible concept applying both to physical and non-physical reality. Growth (again, both physical and psychic) of necessity requires vulnerability to pain: as a defensive mechanism and warning device, as an incentive to development and progenitor of invention and as a fundamental pre-requisite for the forming of relationships invested with sensitivity and awareness of values termed human. Pain has therefore a large and legitimate part to play in the successful progress of growth.

So far so good: but pain and growth play out their particular partnership in the arena of freedom. In this area there are the pressures of need, competition, desire, deprivation and consequent triggering of self-defence and aggression. There is the hazard, the hardship and the caprice of event which freedom throws into the pool of experience. And there is, or some think there is, an unseen power of evil influencing some aspects of the push and drive and response which set events in motion. In any case, and this is for the moment the important point, freedom allows of the impact of pain outside and beyond the terms of its strict necessity for growth. Pain then may wear the face of sin, wielding the weapons of provocation and self-aggrandizement, and issuing in disturbance, damage and destruction, enmity and revenge. You cannot have one face of pain, the large and legitimate one of assisting growth, without the other, the large and illegitimate one of disturbing it. Freedom and growth do not deal in neat and rational categories of smoothly ordered actions and maximum avoidance of pain. Growth is ebullient and explosive, and the higher it ascends in the scale of complexity, the greater and the more unfearing is the freedom with which it expands and experiments.

Now, it is not so far so good; it is so far much better. In whatever way we may choose to interpret evil, and this comes up for some discussion in a later chapter, it is clear from all experience that the impact of pain does indeed far exceed necessity and is inflicted and borne in prodigiously awesome quantity. There is natural disaster, but far more continuously and more subtly there is sin. One person or group, knowingly or blindly, rides roughshod over the needs, interests or sensitivities of another person or group. One person or group, through fear of being hurt or reluctance to risk an involvement in self-sacrifice, closes the channels of communication, withdraws from a need or opportunity, seeks the safety of self at the expense of the suffering of another. One, in short, causes another unnecessary pain. Observing this, men and women question God's goodness or dismiss it as a hoax. Yet here precisely is the dynamic alchemy of the divine wisdom. The pain which seems to contradict love, that same pain which though large and illegitimate you cannot do without, is the very thing which is pressed into service to authenticate and perfect love. The turmoils of our growing into completeness are the very and precise things without which our completeness could not be reached. The pains of our ebullient freedom are the very things, the absolutely necessary things, through which love is sharpened and strengthened and deepened and established and divinized. No love is truly love until it has been proved capable of standing undeterred at the prospect or actuality of pain inflicted by another's disaffection. The apex of the divine wisdom is perceived in the fact that the pains and travails which are inseparable from our growth and development as persons are capable of being re-designed into the means of drawing forth a quality of love which could not, without those pains, come into being. The by-product of growth in freedom becomes the main factor in the stimulation of growth in love. That need be no surprise, since the unwanted by-products of the body's growth become the main factors in the fertilization of the ground-grown things. The second face of pain, the pain which hurts unnecessarily and sinfully, is capable of performing a vital function for spiritual growth. It is the means of calling forth love at a more than natural, in other words super-natural, level, a love which can disregard the pain experienced and can continue to go out undiminished towards the perpetrator. That love which seeks to remain undeterred and undiminished in face of pain is none other than the principal ingredient of for-giveness. Forgiveness is the crowning accomplishment of love, both in God and in man.

That second face of pain is capable of drawing forth this crown-ing act of forgiveness and so enhancing the stature of the for-giver as well as bringing relief to the perpetrator. But it may not do this. Pain has two faces and it can go two ways. It is perfectly possible for it to provoke revenge instead of forgiveness, to exacerbate hatred instead of nurturing love, to play the game of the devil instead of advancing the creativity of God. We put our finger on a central nerve of the meaning of atonement when we see that what Christ accomplished was to embrace the second face of pain and bring it into the God-held, creativity-bearing sphere of experience, alchemizing the whole of it into forgiveness and thus into perfection and glory. If Christ's perfection came through the grasping of pain into the God-held activity of forgiveness, then man's perfection must come in that way too. When at ultimate length this has been accomplished in man's own arena of freedom, the feathers of the dove-tail will have come together and have formed a pattern of elegance which only divine truth can yield.

In Christ's fore-running in the arena of both battle and freedom, he marked out the way and supplied the means of turning the second face to good account; and he forged an instrument of spirit which can bring into the armoury of creativeness every known and unknown caprice to which freedom can give existence.

﹌ 7 ﹌

The End of Evolution

IN ALL IMPORTANT respects evolution is finished for humanity. Powers of brain and body, speech, memory, imagination, rational intellect and physical skills have long been established in all races. It may be that some racial groups are described as 'evolving peoples', but this is a description with a political slant and is a misuse of the word 'evolving' and a misjudgment on the peoples concerned.

All around man, the animal world and the vegetable, the world of germs and viruses and the universe itself, are no doubt still evolving. There the panorama of nature's development continues to provide the key idea lying behind creative progress: and science is busier than ever uncovering the intricate mechanisms of cell, enzyme and chromosome by which nature's survival and self-perpetuation are sustained. But in the midst of it all man has become man and evolution can do no more to make him more truly man than now he is and has been for a long time.

He has come to the end of that phase of his journey; to the end, that is, of evolution's ability to do anything significant for him. Now something new is happening. Alone among all his erstwhile companions in the animal kingdom man had outgrown and left behind the evolution which brought him to where he is. He is the product of it, and his body and mind are structured as they are because of it, but now he has begun to belong predominantly to a dimension outside it and beyond it, and evolution can no longer carry him to his destination.

Separated now by a wide gulf from those erstwhile companions, he is driven more insistently than he often realizes by moral forces of which evolution does not know. His goal is no longer survival; it stretches outwards far beyond and its symptoms are a hunger for righteousness, a concern for justice, a need both to forgive and to be forgiven; and withal a thirst for love and an awareness of God. He stands at the threshold of bigger things than evolution has accomplished in the past or can ever accomplish in the future: bigger than simply becoming more human than before. We come nearer to an understanding of the meaning of man's unrest as we realize that he can never be satisfied at a purely human level because his destiny transcends all that evolution or nature can offer.

It is at this point that there comes a sharp and essential divergence from the line of thinking followed in the celebrated writings of Teilhard de Chardin. In his early work, and specially in *The Phenomenon of Man*, he developed the argument that man's final completion was destined to be reached along the path of continued evolutionary progress. It was this which was the basic and justified reason for the criticisms in Christian circles of Teilhard's position. For evolutionary advance does not leave room for a radical facing of the largest questions with which Christianity is concerned – evil, sin, forgiveness, grace. In brief (and using for once a technical Christian term), evolution can never be a substitute for salvation. To put it in other words, man cannot reach his supernatural destiny by means of nature's processes of development.

Whether or not the end of human evolution is scientifically acceptable (and here there is no competence to judge of such things), strangely enough Christianity offers a confirmation of its own in this direction; one which Teilhard might have detected. Indeed from the religious point of view it places the idea beyond dispute. It is this. It could hardly be regarded as making logical sense that Christ should have come to take his part in human affairs if there still lay ahead for humanity further evolutionary change. For then he could not have spoken and acted with a universal relevance for all time. His coming must have been appointed when he, sharing the nature of *homo sapiens*, could be towards every other *homo sapiens* the source of divine knowledge and the link of divine communication. He did not come to enter world affairs as, for instance, hominoid ape or even a Neanderthal man: for then how could his words and acts speak truly to us who are neither of these things? It is impossible to suppose anything else but that he came as man fully evolved into the estate of *homo sapiens*, when the evolutionary development was finished and its implications settled. Only thus could he communicate the depths of his own divinity to all mankind for all time and in all places.

It was at this point when evolution had bowed out, that that quest for divine awareness which in its varying forms we call religion stepped on to the human stage. In its earliest forms it consisted largely of laws and customs designed to safeguard the cohesion and survival of the tribe or race, and the moral sanction for enforcement was vested in a priest-king with semi-divine status or in persons holding the status of prophet, shaman or witch-doctor. Nevertheless, behind these was the confused awareness of a transcedent presence, often terrifying, who exerted ultimate power. Religion, even in early times, came not aiming to place humanity in a moral straight-jacket but pointing to man's aspiration to be linked with the divine and to be given some kind of participation in the divine favour. Religion points precisely to what evolution cannot do; to what it is not intended to do; to what it has no wish to do.

Evolution is concerned with adaptation and progress in the sphere of physical (and thus instinctive) life, leading the species on in its bid for survival and for greater efficiency. It works on the market forces of supply and demand in such things as aggression, defence, competition, survival of the fittest, might is right. Even the harmonies of ecological balance are purchased at the price of such forces. To say this is not to denigrate evolution and the ecologies and excellences it has produced. It is, after all, the mechanism which has produced the whole intricate structure of man's person and of the environment which supports him.

Religion, on the other hand, is concerned with the search for a spiritual relationship with God and with the gradual discovery of how human and social relationships are to be most fulfillingly maintained. As Christ said, religion is the exacting obligation of a wholehearted love of God and of a selfless love of one's neighbour. The whole story of the Old Testament feels its way by painful and slow degrees towards a realization of this interpretation of love. Love, therefore, is the final and exacting goal of man's religious destiny. And here we begin to see the profound contrast between man as creature of evolution and man as destined for the dimension beyond evolution. For man's aspiration for divine kinship and his quest for love are often in confrontation with what his evolutionary nature would like and with how his natural instincts would prefer to respond. Love in any meaning worthy of the name must yield up aggression, sometimes make itself defenceless, be prepared to be vulnerable, eschew the natural satisfaction of revenge, not ride completely roughshod over its neighbour, must lose in order to gain, die in order to live, bear pain in order to accomplish the supreme act of forgiving. It is from the natural wordly point of view often a madness, a nonsense, a suicide. It challenges our staunchest evolutionary instincts and bids them abandon their self-centred claims, to take second place and even to be annihilated. It is no wonder that men and women make a thousand excuses to dodge its obligation and resist its demands with all their might because so much of man's might is evolutionary, survivalist, self-defensive, competitive. Yet if men and women are to be more than a transient product of evolutionary development, here today and gone tomorrow, these pressures of spirit must come to lift and transform their evolutionary raw materials into a new creation of divine kinship. Here we begin to see what we shall stress again and again: the strange, unique and exacting situation in which humanity finds itself. Alone among all the possessors of flesh and blood, humanity must journey beyond the fringe of what nature lays down as its

normal limits. There lies before us willy-nilly, whether we like it
or not, the pressure of spirit upon nature, the constraint of spiritual demand on evolutionary desire, the claim of the divine upon
all that is human.

No doubt to the great majority of people this pressing in of the
spiritual upon the natural seems to be a tiresome brake exerted
against the vigour of human life-force. It can very easily appear
as a moral straight-jacket attempting to inhibit fun, happiness
success, freedom, human-ness. But no great enterprise is achieved
without the sacrifice of something. The power of spirit has to
eclipse and transcend some of the vigour which evolution has
given, just as man has to transcend the animal kingdom, sacrificing
some of its freedom and eclipsing some of its exuberances. In fact
that which is spiritual is the very opposite of being life-inhibiting
just as human life is far from inhibiting compared with animal
existence. The spiritual dimension confers a wider freedom and an
even greater release of creative energy. Evolutionary vigour
alone, life-force be it never so strong, are not enough for the
human design. These might carry the human race on and on until
some day it was overtaken by extinction as were the dinosaur and
the mammoth; or until it was terminated by the natural evolution
of the solar system as is bound to happen in due course when the
planets and ourselves among them are enveloped in the dying
expansion of the sun. Evolutionary vigour alone in the case of the
individual carries a person onwards and forwards to a decline of
strength and to the certainty of death. When all is said and done
about the scientific view of man, we cannot escape the question
with which religion is concerned, whether the human person is
simply an expendable article here on earth or whether (as religion
says) he and she have a larger and more permanent destiny here-
after.

Life would surely appear as a strangely exacting effort if extinction, and extinction only, lay at the end of it. It could be, as an
intellectual proposition, that that is how things are: many people
believe that it is so. But there are profound intimations at other

levels that that is not the true or complete story. To the Christian
faithful the most powerful evidence is in the resurrection of Christ
and in the incontrovertible fact of perennial faith on the part of
the great multitudes of people. Intellectually the strongest indication is the coherence which can be discerned running through
the whole sweep of events in human affairs: an environment
where life can arise and survive, amid a universe which is probably
almost wholly alien to life: the unbroken chain of survival and
progress of living species: the arrival of man after a prodigious
and hazardous journey through evolution: man's endowment
with qualities of awareness unique among all other species: man's
unending pre-occupation with the moral questions of justice and
truth and his extraordinary attachment to the concept of love. To
say that all this is the consequence of accidental forces in the
universe cannot be described as compelling. When we see how
the component elements of this train of events – the fact of suffering, the quest for love, the presence of evil – all dovetail exactly
into the solution offered by Christianity, it becomes compelling
in the other direction and the ideas of accident and of man's
expendability dissolve into an unsubstantial vapour. Christianity
tells us that beyond the physical rise and fall of solar systems and
planets, moons and mountains, beyond the evolutionary arrival
and disappearance of reptile, bird and mammal, Christ has
established in the *milieu* of humanity a new creation which shall
not be overtaken by the decline and termination of the species
nor extinguished by the natural evolution of the universe. There
are those who, with becoming modesty and in the interest of
truth, question the central importance of man which the Western
world at least has taken for granted. It is hard to find an intelligent
purpose in what we know of the universe if it is not centred on the
drama of the human enterprise and in the vision of things accorded
to us by Christianity, when our physical mode of being has been
extinguished, when possibly the entire universe has passed away;
there will then remain a humanity which cannot pass away because it is no longer evolutionary dust but of divine-humanity

made immortal by kinship with the Creator. As scaffolding becomes eventually expendable in the making of a building, so the
whole evolutionary process will receive its final significance as the
long process of scaffolding which produced man will at some point
be finally and honourably dismantled.

Evolution does not therefore supply in itself a simple answer as
though it were possible to say that mankind will evolve towards
greater goodness, a higher moral sense, towards freedom from
suffering or a more just social organization (although there are
those who pin hopes on such an idea). Evolution as such is finished
and this unfortunately is a vain hope. It does, however, offer us a
trail of illumination on almost every single problem both of our
spiritual quest and of our existential experience. It lays bare the
groundwork, as though in an archaeological excavation, in which
we may trace the underlying role of freedom in the creative purpose, the complete yet comprehensible function of pain and the
relation between pain and love. Of the mysterious intrusion of
evil it yields a more comprehensible account than ever the Garden
of Eden doctrine of original sin could give.

ঞ 8 ৬

Fall and Proliferation

MAN'S EARLIEST origin was not in some splendid perfection of innocence and moral integrity in a far-off Eden. It was in a simple, undiversified cell stirring to the first tremor of livingness chronologically far further away than Eden was ever supposed to have been. Our beginning was not in the heights but out of the depths, and human imagination is not equal to grasping the prodigious journey of selection and complexification which has brought that primaeval speck to the physical and psychic intricacy of man with his technological skills and his morally self-conscious rationality.

It is more for the anthropologist than for the theological thinker to say things about what was happening in that prodigious journey while our forebears were passing from the state of pre-man into the status of *homo sapiens*. No doubt it was a long and hazardous passage of which the stages of advance were imperceptibly slow. No doubt much of the detail will remain a matter of speculation for everyone including the anthropologist. However, it is legitimate for the amateur to guess that, as that indistinct and long-drawn-out threshold was being crossed, there began to dawn that first light of rational self-conscious thought and the first signs of an embryonic moral faculty. Whatever some enthusiasts may say about animal behaviour betraying certain hints of humanity and of moral-style qualities, it seems unarguable that animal life in general does not contain rational moral self-consciousness and that man, as he emerged into history in the estate of *homo sapiens*, certainly did. Somewhere along the line, if indeed our species did arise out of animal origins, this transition must have taken place.

It was mankind's first crucial threshold of advance towards his destiny. There was another threshold to come, that of his entry into the possession of love, our concern here. The passing of the first was, of necessity, a matter of immense output of effort, but the second of the two, the travail of entry into love, was to be the greatest, and it is still going on.

At the same time, man had brought with him into his newly-won estate all the evolutionary equipment which had served his progress so well and for so long: need, desire, fear, acquisitiveness and protectiveness, the instinct of survival and the instinct of procreation and many others, all dovetailed into the two major attributes of aggression and defence. These were already embedded in his emotional and instinctive make-up. They were as necessary as ever, in fact more necessary, for the safeguarding of his increasingly complex needs and sensitivities; and they were as ready as ever, in fact more ready, to be touched into action by a threat to his security or by the kindling of some desire. A huge world was opening before man in which his vulnerability was extending from the physical sphere into one which was far more difficult to assess or predict, the inner world of mental and emotional sensitivity, the central area of that most delicate thing, selfhood.

All these weapons belonging to the evolutionary armoury, which had at an earlier stage worked at an exclusively instructive and non-moral level, were available to be used now in purposeful ways for personal ends. Aggressions and defensivenesses remained in large part impulsive and passionate – they are widely so today – but they could, when needed, be thought out and calculated. At the same time as man's vulnerabilities were extending, he was also discovering an alluring extension of his power to promote his own interests and indulge his wishes.

At what stage of development moral awareness and the faculty of conscience began to appear is again a matter of surmise. Moral awareness must be a product of the ability of rational consciousness to perceive cause and effect, act and consequence. Conscience seems to be fostered by a subtle interaction between the fear of painful consequence and the prospect of pleasant reward. Animals can be trained to the possession of primitive degrees of conscience by the use of these pressures. These pressures form an essential part of the moral shaping of children and, whatever anyone may say, the fear of punishment and the pleasure of approval are not only salutary and legitimate but are essential parts of a human person's moral equipping. With the human, however, in distinction from the animal, the process of conscience-building and moral-equipping has infinite scope for being deepened through rational thought and spiritual instruction. In humans conscience can and should be educated, and its education must be directed towards the perception of ends which are in tune with the growing spiritual awareness.

For St Paul this coming to life of moral awareness and of conscience was connected with the formulation of the old law of Judaism. But evidence from legal systems and civil enactments in other societies as well as from primitive religions in widely varying stages of development shows that conscience and moral awareness have been universal attributes of human kind from early times. Here we are not concerned with religious discussion but with a fact of human life; what matters is that somehow and at some period men and women found within themselves the beginnings of a sense of moral sanction. They did things and knew that those things were good; and they did things, perceived their ill effects and yet went on doing them. Simple, instinctive, non-moral aggressions and defensivenesses became known, sometimes calculated, morally-coloured actions. Long ages before St Paul they experienced what later made St Paul despair. Knowing that they should not, they did; and knowing that they should, they did not. For the first time, as the Genesis account correctly surmises, man knew good and evil.

It was in some such train of events as this that fall – if we must call it fall – may be diagnosed. It was something which emerged as an inevitable corollary of the onward movement of evolution and psychic progress at a particularly crucial stage in mankind's development. It was a further stage of that first threshold over which man entered upon his humanity. This was no fall from perfection, for there was no perfection and no height from which to fall. It was no tearing asunder of mankind's relationship with God, for he can have had only the most rudimentary awareness of the numinous. It can have brought no wholesome condemnation on man because he was groping his evolutionary way forward and learning, as a child learns, a more exacting use of his evolutionary equipment. Above all, this was no cataclysmic moral tragedy, as Christian thought has felt obliged in the past to depict it, because through these events man was moving further into moral awareness, not away from it. It was the introduction to his quest for God, not the shutting of the door upon that quest; his baptism into the travail of entry into love, not his rejection of a supposedly existing capacity to love.

There are other interpretations of fall which explain it as the existential, contemporary, individual kicking over the traces on the part of each particular person. But such ideas are not essentially different from the more traditional ones taken from the Genesis story. They still depict man as having once known God and as having culpably fallen away from him; and God as having, by moral necessity, excluded man from his favour and as having to take special action through Christ in order to restore the broken relationship. They picture forgiveness, incidentally, as restoring a person to relationship with God: whereas very frequently such repentance and forgiveness afford the very first opportunity a person has ever had to be brought into that relationship. There remains the supposition that, if man had not been so wicked, the special intervention by Christ, with all that it entailed, might never have had to take place. This is quite different from a view in which fall is seen as a natural implication of the progress of the divine plan through evolution and seen, moreover, as the means and the spur of man's baptism in the fire of moral awareness and of his momentous venturing out into the exacting arena of spiritual freedom. We need no longer visualize God as being taken, as it

were, disagreeably by surprise at the turn of events, nor Christ as
having to mend a near hopeless situation in his world. We shall
not, either, have to be concerned with theories which bend backwards or forwards to work out how the sacrifice of Christ pro-
pitiated the Father and enabled him to restore alienated man to
his favour. There is no profit in wishful speculation about 'if only':
if only man had not made such a mess of things; if only God had
not created man with such a propensity to be wicked. The only
truth is what is, and it is idle to think that God might have organized his creation in any other way. It is interesting that while
theology has made so strong an insistence on man's depravity
and damnation – much stronger than can be supported by Jesus'
words – the man in the street has, probably unconsciously, replied
with his doubts about the justice, wisdom and goodness of God.
It ought now to be more possible than before to do more balanced
justice to God and man. This will happen so soon as we portray
Christ's coming as an integral part of the whole sweep of the
creative enterprise and see his ordeal as the conquest and the
drawing into new creative use of elements which, not by divine
permission only but by divine necessity, had been given a wild and
sometimes fractious freedom.

It would, however, be an incomplete diagnosis to depict this
as no more than an evolutionary moment; as a process at a natural
level which accompanied man's progress into a higher psychic
key. Such a description (which is in fact authentic at a biological
and psychological level) would not allow to this threshold the
crucial and dramatic quality it possesses. For something very
radical was beginning to take place in the unfolding of creation,
far transcending the more obvious outer layer of events. Man
was coming to the fringe of that spiritual world in which the significance of his existence was to lie. His progress was taking him
forward, not merely into greater ranges of human efficiency or
intelligence, nor on an evolutionary advance, but into an arena in
which issues of eternal spiritual consequence were to be decided.
And the result, affecting God's purpose and man's own destiny,

was to be brought to its decisive denouement inside man himself. Waiting, as it were, at the side, while man uncertainly stretched out his own wings of awareness and freedom, were the contenders for man's future: God, in love, to give man the kingdom prepared for him, and Satan, in envy, to destroy man lest he should gain that prize. No dualism, this, for God alone created. The demon has no power of creation, only of perversion and destruction. Yet were it not for the freedom which enabled man's entry into love and which at the same time permits love's opposite to work, the depths of God's love could not be shown, nor could man receive the grace which confers upon him a participation in divine nature. It would be possible to describe the human phenomenon as purely human and the 'fall' as merely a natural process; but then we should be robbed of the possibility of making an intelligible synthesis of God's love and man's troubles, of Christ's incarnation and man's crowning with glory.

If we are to perceive the extent of these issues and to make satisfactory surveying and mapping of the real character of the terrain of man's 'fall' and of the world's disarrays, we have first to return to the question of evil and to come to terms with its realities. It is a fallacy widespread today in the Western world that thought and behaviour are determined by the brain and by the intellect, that one has only to educate people sufficiently and point out what is right, good, sensible and virtuous, for them to do it. It is a fallacy of thinking that humans are guided by the rational mind whereas in fact they are driven by passions and feelings far below the coolness of reason. Why else do we talk about 'emotive' statements, if it were not that man's acts and thoughts are coloured from sensitive psychological and spiritual sources? If he were a brain-man, a rational creature, it would be reasonable to think that morality would be a matter of trial and error, so that errors once (or twice) made would be realized and eliminated.

But experience tells us that that is simply not the case; and that the propensity to wrong-doing is deeper and more persistent than that. Even if you discount St Paul's self-disappointment in 'The good that I would I do not: but the evil which I would not, that I do', you will still find it very hard to justify the unending and damaging behaviour of some people and organizations as rational. Anyone, moreover, who has struggled with recurring temptation and repeated remorse after wrong-doing (and that is everyone except a few totally amoral people) knows that one cannot simply think them or decide them out of existence. They come with greater power than that of natural reasoning; otherwise natural reasoning could decide against them. And it doesn't.

People sometimes do not want to rid themselves of things they know are wrong, even though they hate the remorse which comes afterwards. This can sometimes be because of an insistent demand for freedom or fulfilment which has been thwarted or denied, which they do not know how to fulfil in any other way. It can thus be a quite understandable exercise in survival or self-respect. But behind this much more than freedom is at work. For if I can perceive a particular use of freedom to be destructive or guilt-ridden, why should I not, why so often can I not, be in command of it? And why, if I am the child of God, should I like the destructiveness, the selfishness, the lust? There can only be the explanation that behind this fractious use of freedom is a power of spirit, not God's, which is capable of gaining some purchase on my emotions and my will and thus my actions, and which being spirit against my flesh, is stronger than me, as far as my own self, without God's spirit, is concerned. Without going as it were cap in hand to God's grace, I cannot step away from it nor cure myself of it. What, then, is this spirit power which can fasten itself to my will and corrupt my outlook and my actions?

Christian belief has, from its beginnings, ascribed to evil an objective reality and an origin in a personal, conscious, spiritual being. It has become popular in some circles to suppose that modern man need no longer take such things seriously. But an ancient belief having the divine sanction of Christ's own un-doubting acceptance is not to be easily discarded. The reality of the devil and of his demonic intelligence is taken for granted in the present discussion and, from the synthesis which this discussion suggests, it appears that he exists not by divine permission alone but by the necessities of the whole creative process. That process is not a small parochial matter of comfort, smoothness and absence of challenge: it is one in which the greatness of man's spiritual stature may only emerge in confrontation with a spiritual power far beyond his human means to overcome.

We have now to attempt to establish some kind of theory of how the devil obtains his leverage on mankind's soul and mankind's conduct. Only when this is done will it be possible to trace how that domination over man is maintained, how it is extended by the effect of vicious circles, and how its proliferation is defeated by forgiveness – wherein the focus of atonement is found.

The devil has no point of leverage in the world save through the medium of man's vulnerability of flesh and mind. Evil remains invisible until the emotions are touched, the mind is engaged, the will is moved and hand or tongue translate responses of fear, anger, greed, desire or revenge into action. Even if the evangelist has recorded a true, rather than an imaginary, tail-piece to the story of the Gadarene demoniac (and I think it is imaginary), his account supports the idea that man alone fulfils the devil's needs. The Gadarene swine could do nothing more malign than rush down a slope into the sea. They had no psychic equipment with which to respond in a calculated way to demonic pressures. Only in mankind, with his developed self-consciousness and his possession of mind and will, does there exist the effective agency through which evil intention can be crystallized into evil hard fact. And only in man is it the devil's desire to do this, for it is man whom he wants to corrupt and over whom he designs to maintain his domination.

In the long evolutionary prelude to man's advent on earth, no doubt the devil awaited the time when there would arrive this combination of consciousness and will – this accessibility of spiritual life – through which to gain his foothold in the human arena. From there he could crystallize his own consciously-

willed malice into practical fact and weave his web of interacting
evil around man's relationships. Perhaps already he 'went to and
fro in the earth and up and down in it' as he perceived more and
more clearly the unique and irrevocable destiny of man to par-
take ultimately of divine nature. As he watched man's powers
advance, no doubt he began to see the radical vulnerabilities
which so delicate a destiny contained, and he looked for the soft
spots where his strategy would best succeed. C. S. Lewis in
The Screwtape Letters created a vivid picture of the demon's disgust
at the fact that man, the earth-born, earth-fed creature, made not
of pure spirit but of flesh, should have been chosen out of the
whole creation for so exalted a spiritual end, exalted above the
angels. But it was not until man had passed over the threshold
into true humanity that the devil had his point of purchase where
he could begin to work his will. Then he could penetrate man's
inner being and search for an opportunity to destroy his potential
sonship of God. This is the theme of the opening scene of the
drama played out in the book of Job, though 'the Satan' there is
not what later ages came to call 'the devil'.

In humanity, the devil had a whole range of physical and mental
reactions readymade for his exploitation, nurtured and sharpened
over untold ages of evolutionary advance and struggle. It was, and
is, the perfect material for temptation. Aggressive and defensive
instincts – desires, needs, fears, anxieties and angers – were woven
into the texture of his human make-up. They were essential for
his survival and their roots ran into the depths of his being and
back down the long corridor of his ancestry. At any moment the
devil could galvanize these into action in a thousand variations:
suggesting desires and pointing out needs and threatening that
their non-fulfilment may be intolerable; playing on old resentments and bringing new – and often unfounded – suspicions to
mind; exaggerating differences and oppositions; twisting words;
deterring from duty because of the risk of self-sacrifice; luring to
illicit fulfilments because of the fear of deprivation of happiness.
Moreover, as man became more sophisticated, his needs and

desires increased and it was possible to deceive him into thinking
that the yearnings of his now stirring spiritual capacity should be
fulfilled through the familiar channels of his biological being.
Self-aggrandizement and self-fulfilments were capable of being
fed from sources which should properly impel him towards their
opposites; thus aggression and defence and competitiveness
could be exacerbated on the grand scale.

What, one must ask, was the prime means of setting these
reactions into motion? What was the soft spot – or the exposed
nerve – where the evil strategy was to have its effective leverage?

It emerges quite clearly that this is pain and always will be
pain, while this present dispensation continues. Out of the whole
armoury of evolutionary equipment with which sentient life is
endowed, it is the one sufficient weapon which the demon could
choose with which to make himself the arbiter of man's conduct.
It lies at the deepest level of experience and is the most ancient
and, for very good reasons, the most dreaded element in that
experience. Being designed by nature to protect and deflect its
owners from dangerous things and to lure them towards needed
things, in the interests of survival, it is the perfect tool ready-made
for the demon to use for precisely the same purposes. With it he is
able to deflect a person from duty, in smallest detail or largest
principle, and with it he can lure a person to the fulfilment of a
desire by the threat or prospect that that duty will be painful. He
may (in regard to large principle) deter a man from allowing himself to accept the reality of God and of Christian faith through the
suggestion that that acknowledgment would involve consequences not only of tiresome duty but, perhaps more, of painful
deprivations. He may (as to small detail) cause a person to perpetrate some paltry lie or deceit lest the doing away with it should
expose the personality to the painfulness of derision, criticism or
sense of inferiority. He may lure man or woman to wrong satisfaction or illicit fulfilments by harping on dissatisfaction or
jealousies or by presenting to the imagination the joy of some particular indulgence. But even this comes to the same thing in the

end. If one says with St James that the strategy of the demonic is
to lure a person to the conceiving of lust so that it brings forth
death, I have to reply that behind that lust is something stronger –
nothing less than the big stick of the pictured pain of deprivation
of non-fulfilment of desire, of the thwarting of will and the frustration of intention. Refuse a baby what it wants and it bursts
into tears; take away a toy from a child and the same thing
happens. Behind every desire is the ever-present threat of the
pain of deprivation. Ask yourself what is the crux of resisting
temptation; and surely the answer is the prospect of bleakness
and deprivation at the non-fulfilment of that desire. The pain of
deprivation, even more than the fulfilment of having, is the ultimate sanction by which a person is driven to cross from temptation to sin.

Thirdly, with it he succeeds in doing damage which has the
subtlest consequences and the most widespread effects of all.
Where there has been hurt or misunderstanding between people
and where a human relationship has been damaged, he will pre-
vent the one from making apology or acknowledgment and the
other from being willing to forgive and so mend the hurt. Here,
in both cases, hurt has to be borne in order to undo hurt. And in
putting pressure on both to maintain pride and isolation, in saving
them from one hurt, he greatly multiplies the hurt which first did
the harm.

Pain is the agent by which the multiplicity of man's thoughts,
words and deeds are turned into that selfishness which is called
sin; that movement of the will which refuses the good and em-
braces the evil because to do otherwise would be a (seemingly)
intolerable painfulness. It is the force which makes him choose
the marginally less good or the marginally more evil, the line of
least resistance instead of the line of self-sacrifice; the line of least
effort; least risk, least discomfort; of greatest satisfaction, greatest
profit, greatest safety. Above all it is the deterrent to the humbling
act of repentance and the self-giving act of forgiveness.

It might seem to be enough to have dug down and unearthed, in the form of pain, a kind of tap-root out of which human conduct draws its deepest impulse; the piece of evolutionary equipment which, while basically belonging to God's creative purpose and having essential functions in it, can be used by evil to browbeat man into wrong-doing. It does indeed go some way towards explaining mankind's general disarray and individual man's confusion of purpose, his conscious sins and his irrational violence. It helps us to understand why man so easily chooses the lesser good or the greater evil, the line of least resistance or of greater selfishness: and why he displays reluctance to choose a path of self-sacrifice, self-involvement and self-giving. At the same time it throws light on one essential aspect of the passion and crucifixion of Christ, in the fact that Christ embraced pain in order to make the experience his own preserve, to wrest it from the demon's control and to bring the totality of it back into the creative resources of God. This was, after all, the elemental region in which Christ made his confrontation with the stronghold of evil. For if pain can so effectively be used as arbiter of conduct for evil, there was no alternative to its having to be won as potential creative power for good. This aspect is not for discussion now, but will be treated later on in reference to the defeat of evil.

Nevertheless, to see pain as simply the trigger-point underlying man's sins, negligences and ignorances – as the deterrent to good and the provocation to evil – is nowhere near to being the whole story. We have to dig, not deeper, but more widely, to trace and discover how evil spreads its tentacles of power and how it maintains its hold on the world. St John does not exaggerate when he says that the whole world lies in the evil one. The evil one has a vantage point in every human personality, and from all of them he weaves an interlacing web of efficacy through human emotions – individual, group and national. When the reality of this machination and the depth at which it operates are understood, then it becomes possible to see forgiveness in the central position of importance which Christ himself, the gospels, subsequent theology and much human experience have given it,

and it also becomes clear how forgiveness is the cardinal factor
in the defeat of evil. It is often thought that the defeat of evil lies in
social, political, economic, medical and psychological pro-
grammes: and of course they have a necessary function in the
world. But at the depth at which evils, enmities, hatreds, jealousies
and angers proliferate, there is only one thing which avails, and
that is the confrontation of pain by love and the alchemistic
activity that emerges from this confrontation, which is forgiveness, forgiveness that is to say, not only from God but from man
to man. To the arrogant its solvent power may be unperceived,
yet it is the only one. For the arrogant, love is absent and painfulnesses remain intact.

The way in which the demon succeeds in weaving a web of
evil around and within humanity is very simple and all too familiar
to us humans. The natural response of unregenerate man to
feeling he has been hurt is to hit back and hurt back. That salves
his own pain, gives him the spurious sense of justice, of 'getting
even', and makes him feel more secure against future attack from
the same quarter. Revenge, to our evolutionary nature, is sweet.
Yet if this action seems to have put things right, it has really done
the opposite. The pain of the first wrong-doing has in fact been
thrown back at the original offender and has become the provocation for a further onslaught. The grand total of pain and of
consequent evil has increased, and no one can tell how far its
effects may ripple outward from the two people (or groups) concerned. Pain gives birth to sin and sin to pain; aggression rallies
defence and defence passes into aggression (because the best
method of defence is attack). A hurts B and B hurts back; A's
feelings are exacerbated and he in turn takes revenge on B until
soon they are so far apart that neither wants, or is able, to see the
other's point of view. So the hurts, injustices and angers ripple
outwards, touching others as they go, in a typical vicious circle;
and evil proliferates like malignant cells in the body.

The course of events will not, in practice, be so direct and
clear-cut as that, nor so limited as appears when using an example

of two individuals. Not only visible aggressions are inflicted by
one on another but the subtlest pressures, meant or unmeant,
touch deep-laid sensitivities. It may be whole groups suffering
under a sense of injustice or a threat to security who will be provoked to violence, in which individuals may be small centres of
vicious circles within the larger emotional framework. Sometimes
A may not know he has hurt B and may therefore be deeply in-
censed when B's unexpected anger takes him unawares. Certainly the aggressions and defences are, in civilized man, far
more often invisible than visible, psychic than physical; and being
so are more deadly. Aggression may be a purposeful setting aside
of love for the sake of anger and of the desire to hurt; defence
may be a purposeful withdrawing of love for the sake of cruelty
and of the intention of revenge. There is no limit to the variations
in which these processes take place. Always good is the loser, sin
the gainer; and always pain is increased and evil proliferates.

Such is the way of our unregenerate, natural, evolutionary
responses. Mercifully man is not solely unregenerate, natural and
evolutionary. He is made in the image of God and is created to be
a recipient of grace. Therein lies much of the tension of his being,
much of his essential submission to discipline which his nature
hates, much of his striving for moral values. Nothing is more true
than that the flesh wars against the spirit and the spirit against the
flesh and that the two are contrary the one to the other. For the
flesh means our whole evolutionary being with all its drives:
good, bad and indifferent; creative, destructive and simply
necessary. And the spirit means, essentially, love in its illuminat-
ing, directing and sanctifying operation. It may sometimes seem
to man that it is his ill luck, though it is in fact his unique glory, to
be placed amid so great tensions, opportunities and dangers.

Were man not a recipient of grace and were he only an evolutionary being, yet having the power he has, there would be no
exit whatever for him from his imprisonment within the actions
and reactions of his natural self. He would be vulnerable to the
contagions and infections of evil and to the promptings of his and

everyone else's provocativenesses. The evil one would possess
man's conduct and man's soul for ever: no amount of evolutionary
advance could lead to any kind of utopia. The proliferation of
evil would spin each individual into an enclosed cocoon as a
spider spins a fly which it has caught in its web.

Evil depends upon its own independent manipulation of pain.
Christ brought love, that man might enter into the eternal possession of it. In the overcoming of pain, he made that entry possible
and in the forging of forgiveness he created the sole weapon
that could break the vicious circle and ensure the ultimate defeat
of evil.

Freedom Unambiguously Free

FREEDOM IS fundamental to the whole idea of life, humanity and personality. Perhaps only those who have been deprived of it can really appreciate how essential it is. Yet freedom has sometimes, in religious thinking, come rather near to being cast in the role of the villain, the scape-goat on whose shoulders must be laid the responsibility for the existence of evil and sin. 'Free-will', someone might say 'is the real root of the problem; but then, I suppose, we could not do without it', and the problem is often left like that with a faint feeling that free-will is rather a pity. We could, indeed, not do without it. But freedom is a far greater and grander conception than is conveyed by that kind of thought. We should, indeed, not exist without it. It alone can permit growth and development, and nurture human beings and draw forth moral qualities and make people for eternity. Only in freedom can the crucial thing take place which distinguishes man as man and which places him already on the fringes of divinity, that is, man's entry into the experience of love. We must examine what this thing consists of which lies so close to the creative purpose and see what an illumination it throws on our human condition and on our understanding of God.

Freedom does not exist independently as a thing in itself as, for instance, space exists whether or not there are objects to fill it. Freedom only comes into being when there are, not objects to fill it, but living wills to exercise it. There is no freedom except where there are wills capable of making choices and permitted to do so. There is no freedom on the moon, for there are no wills to exercise freedom (except those of rare astronauts; and the freedom they have is limited by the alien nature of the environment). There was no freedom on earth until life first stirred into being. It must have been infinitesimal in extent until time brought greater complexity and a larger range to consciousness. In the primitive animal kingdom it remained limited to the freedom through which instinctual drives were fulfilled – hunting, eating, guarding territory, mating.

With the coming of man after prodigious processes of freedom's experiment, freedom had taken a stride forward. The variety of actions and the range both of thought and of movement were hugely increased. As man grew in psychic power and physical skill, leaving the animal world far behind, so did the freedom originating within him increase. There was formed around him a kind of arena in which his freedom operated, a sphere in which the influence of his will and motive were felt. This freedom arena was simply as large and as small, as extended and as limited, as the range and the size of his growing consciousness. It formed, fanned out and expanded around his widening touch with his world and his mastering of problems, his questing and questioning about the nature of things, his desiring and obtaining of a larger and larger range of knowledge and satisfaction. But this was always against obstacles physical and moral.

The freedom surrounding man's activity is the product of life and uniquely of human life. Annihilate humanity and freedom almost disappears. Withdraw life and freedom is no longer there. The important thing for this enquiry is that man, owing to his growing possession of consciousness, has produced this freedom, has demarcated this unique arena of his own developing and choosing and discovering of his destiny. Man alone is permitted to enter and move in it, for he alone has the capacity to do so. Animals move on its fringe, unaware of its meaning. They are excluded from knowledge of the whys and wherefores of mankind's existence and of his crucial entry into love. Angels and other spiritual beings (so we believe) possess a clarity of awareness for the functions they perform and for the commands they

carry out, but are excluded from immediate experience of man's
joy and travail. They are not called upon to experience the destiny
which man finds so hard, the submission to flesh and blood and the
submergence under pain and sin for the sake of entering love and
of emerging into the grace and freedom of sons of God. They may
even not be admitted to complete understanding of man's cosmic
role, for 'these things the angels desire to look into'. This freedom
(though it is provided by God as the ground work of his desired
plan) is man's freedom and its purpose is man's purpose. If it were
not so, the incarnation would not have been in the flesh and mind
of man. He is charged with the ultimate conquest of it in order
that every aspect of the freedom arena shall be won for God and
held for God. It is his special field of spiritual struggle and warfare,
and in it his own supernatural destiny stands at stake to be won
or lost and the kingdom of heaven to be established 'within' and
therefore 'on earth'. And it was into this arena of man's endeavouring that Christ came to enable man to finish the creation which
neither evolution nor man's endeavouring could make complete.

It would be impossible to exaggerate either the uniqueness of
man's position in the freedom arena which he has created, or the
profoundity of the drama of his journey towards sonship of the
Creator and participation in divine nature. There may be other
places in the universe where man is evolving or has evolved. One
may most certainly think and hope that there are. If so, there is a
similar uniqueness and a similar drama. The drama lies in the fact
that man, developing through untold ages of hazard and effort,
partaking of all the pains and ills and imperfections which growth
and freedom presuppose and produce, flesh born of flesh, subject
to death and to the violence of the elements and the sharpness of
tooth and claw, is destined to receive citizenship of another
dimension, to become partaker of divine inheritance, to be perfected in love, to possess eternal life. All of this is bestowed and
laid hold on, given and possessed, through the medium of flesh and
blood; striven for, struggled with, created and made real. Freedom is the ground of its possibility and also the area of struggle

and overcoming, for it produces all the caprice and hazard, ill, pain and sin which must be alchemized by God's grace into spiritual possession. This earth-born creature is unique and alone in being recipient of the grace which imparts divine life, translates the death-prone into the life-bearing and carries him to the threshold of the divine dimension of love. It is an awesome journey, prodigious in extent. Man alone, not animals, not angels, traverses its length and its depth.

In the dawning of consciousness of early man (so we may surmise, for we are looking below the levels where not even anthropology can tell us things with certainty) and in his discovery of self-conscious will with its uses and effects, man must have gradually crossed a second threshold into the arena of moral freedom. From the simple, instinctive, non-moral – and very limited – freedom of animal life, he passed to a new style of freedom with deeper awareness if his ability to affect the course of life, to do things which he could perceive had consequences either for himself or other people. The horizons began to be filled with more opportunity, more consequence and greater danger. This awareness of consequences was perhaps only a very embryonic ancestor of the developed moral conscience of modern man. Long psychic development would have to be undergone before it could be said that the new horizon denoted a knowledge of good and evil. Nevertheless, at long last, man was, by the very fact of self-consciousness and moral awareness, ready to come in touch with, and be accessible to, the world of the spiritual. The confines of the freedom arena were beginning to extend towards a sphere more strange, powerful and alarming than any till then encountered.

This was a crucial threshold, yet it was the logical extension of the earlier threshold which man crossed from plain consciousness to self-consciousness. It evidently required a high degree of psychic advance for there to be the possibility of the comprehension of spiritual ideas. But there is no hard and fast line marking this threshold. Before early man was able to comprehend intellectually the concept of spirit, he had no doubt begun to be accessible to spiritual influence at the intuitive level: all was imperceptible gradualness of growth. In man's instinctive, emotional, make-up there existed already, formed over the millennia of his evolution from more primitive and vulnerable forebears, all the ingredients around which his spiritual developments were to start taking place.

Man's freedom had come to the level where it touched and was accessible to spiritual influence. He was aware of the experience of well-being and of the general feeling of goodness. He must also have been aware of their opposites, more localized in such things as fear of the numinous, sickness, the power of magic and death. At one end of the spectrum of spirit he could begin to perceive the Creator Spirit and to some extent respond to it. At the other end he is prey to the destroyer spirit representing evil: that which we call the devil.

Something has been said in an earlier chapter about the devil and the reality of demonic spirit powers, and more will have to be said later in this inquiry. There are clergymen and ministers of religion who do not find themselves able to credit the existence of the demonic, but they probably form a small minority in the context of the present and past of Christendom and of the world outside Christendom. For the purposes of the account being given here the reality of the devil is accepted as undeniable for three (among other) reasons. If freedom is truly freedom, there is no logical reason why the spirit world should not contain malign as well as benign occupants. Events in the freedom arena, and specially those to do with Christ's own interpretation of his death and resurrection, would be un-understandable in the context of God's love were it not for outright enmity at a spiritual level more powerful than man's spirit. Evidence from scripture, from occult practice and from the experiences of those called to deal with disturbed or obsessed persons cannot easily be discounted. If we are to see the meaning of Christ's ministry at any but a rather superficial level, it is necessary to consider the demon not just as

tempter but as subverter, subjugator and destroyer; and the grace
emanating from Christ's personal conquest of the personal devil
as the only source of man's safety. Man cannot alone overcome
his danger of subversion. That can only come in identification
with God's love in Christ.

Now that man had begun to come of age, it was as though
these two waited in the wings to woo, lure, claim, capture the
human race. God, Creator, Life-giver, Author, to whom the
world by right belongs, waited to woo through free response the
loved creature which was destined to share not his glory only but
even his divinity. The devil, destroyer, death-dealer, life-hater,
waited to catch the creation in any snare which might drag it
backwards towards the nothingness from which it had been born.
Man's coming near to maturity signalled the beginning of his
entry into the cosmic struggle which was the sole means of his
admission into his spiritual status and destiny. This might be said
another way round. Man's coming to maturity signalled the
beginning of the cosmic spiritual struggle which was to fulfil the
purpose of creation, because that struggle could take place only
in the freedom arena and only in man's flesh-and-blood life where
are the raw materials to which both God and devil have access.
There is the ground of your drama, the drama of struggle in high
places.

Despite his capacity of will and his gift of freedom, man's
nature is born out of earth and rooted in flesh and blood and therefore has no power to contend with forces in the spiritual field.
Man's predicament (and opportunity) is that he is open to influences which are stronger than himself. This is right because
man is not God: he is not creator spirit but created flesh. But it
means also that he cannot dominate the spirit forces of evil. Yet
these are precisely what he must prevail over if in the end the
'freedom of the sons of God' is to become his own possession. So
very rightly has Christianity always insisted that man cannot of
his own strength prevail nor cross the threshold into his divine inheritance. 'Without me you can do nothing,' the Christ said; and

St Paul, 'not of ourselves, it is the gift of God.' If it were not for
this necessary spiritual struggle in freedom man would not lay
hold on the grace which gives eternal life. It is a heresy to say
that man has an immortal soul as though he were by nature invested with a ready-made spirit of divine substance. Man has a
soul that is capable of immortality. That is the truth about him,
and he does truly stand to win or lose this potentiality as he does
or does not give access to God's grace.

That also is why God has made himself ready from before the
foundation of the world to take his place within the creature process, to set his own hand to a further stage of man's creation in
Christ. Man, too, is ready because his selfhood is developed and
his quest for spiritual destiny begun. The Old Testament bears
witness to man's increasing need and expectation of God's
personal presence. Now God must, in Christ, enter into the arena
of freedom, the arena of hazard and hardship, accident and
caprice, of demon-influence and evil and of man's sin, to win it
and hold it for God's creative plan, to forge a supremacy of love
which could stand fast in face of every caprice and every sin and
every pain. He must stand in man's situation, in man's dangerous
freedom, and there establish an unarguable supremacy of God's
spirit which must be drawn upon by man in the travail of his own
entry into love. That supremacy, it will be seen, must be the
supremacy of love in face of all that might, in any conceivable
circumstances, assail it: love which stands and remains un-
changeable. This, too, man must appropriate at length for the
establishment of the kingdom.

God is, in one sense, indigenous to his own creation. The Word
of God, (without him, St John says, was not anything made that
was made), the Logos, is the principle of its order and orderliness.
By him it was made, in it he presides, and in its coherence he is
perceived. This ordered creation, the continuity and stability of
which is the necessary condition for man's existence and progress,
is the womb from which man emerges and steps out towards his
entry into freedom, consciousness and ultimate love. Man arose

from it, is part of it, is made and nurtured out of it. Yet as he arises
from it, with his flesh and blood still carrying the continuity and
stability of the background, his qualities of mind and spirit out-
strip the ordered creation and rise into a new sphere of being. In
that new sphere of being man has broken away in the freedom of
his inward self from the controlling orderliness of the Logos, of
that divine creativity which commands the universe to stand fast,
the crystal to form, the cabbage to grow green and the robin to
beget a robin.

His freedom of soul and spirit must take on a new, different
orderliness, one that is a kingdom within himself and spreads a
kingdom around himself. There must be a new forging of invisible order, the creating of a new kingdom in man and in man's
arena of freedom. But God must, of absolute necessity, do this
new creating and this new ordering from within the arena in
which freedom exists and in which man chooses, responds and
acts. Were he to influence or to manipulate the stream of freedom
from 'outside', he would be maiming the very freedom which is
essential to his purpose and interfering with the special character
of man's ascent to spiritual stature. The stress of human freedom
can only be modified, enlarged or restrained by the choice of the
will within that freedom. That is the nature of human responsibility, and it is the nature of the challenge through which man may
lay hold of his spiritual opportunity or let it pass him by. It must
be by his choice, choice of good or choice of evil, otherwise a
person is a machine, computer or automaton. God influences but
does not force (while the demon will use any subtlety or force to
lure or browbeat, as we shall see), because God desires love and
love cannot be other than by free response. This is the crucial
point in any discussion of 'why God allows . . .' or 'why God does
not do anything about . . .'

The Logos, although indigenous to that which is his own,
could not enter to begin the new creation in man until man himself had reached the point of development where he could respond
to the divine initiative. Certainly he could not enter in the lowlier

stages of creation, for he could not represent God in substance of
a star, a crystal, a cabbage or a robin: in these he was present
already as the principle of their existence. He could only come
where there was moral and spiritual freedom and already the
potentiality of a response of love and a kindling of godlikeness.
He could only come a person, among persons, born of the substance of one such as Mary his Mother. Not until freedom had
spread out from man's consciousness to touch the confines of
spirit could the Logos come to his creation as the Christ. But when
freedom had come, then it was necessary and unavoidable that he
should come, should be born in man's arena of freedom, in the
flesh where his destiny was being worked out and striven for.
Before, he could not. Now he must. Incarnation of the word was
eternally part of God's purpose in making provision for man's
entry into love.

The need of freedom is an ultimate necessity for living things,
and its withdrawal brings members of the animal world near to
the basic fear of annihilation – as witness the terrified panting of a
bird when caught in the hand. Even more is freedom essential to
the condition of being human, for the need of it runs from the
animal-linked instinct through to consciousness with all its complexity of mind, spirit, emotion and will. The human therefore
fights, like the animal but with increased power, to overcome a
threat to his or her freedom; and gives it up only with the utmost reluctance. In the relation to God, the human finds himself
willing to yield freedom only when it is perceived that an extended and enhanced freedom is held out, and to those who enter
into such a relation. This principle holds good at a purely human
level. Men and women will, to a certain degree, give away their
freedom in the interests of love, and may, if they are fortunate,
find that their freedom has been not diminished but increased.
Love not only gives away its own freedom but in so doing be-
stows liberation on the one who is loved.

This is the human-sized pattern of the extended freedom held
out to mankind by God and offered to Anglicans in the second

collect for Morning Prayer in the not immediately inspiring words
'whose service is perfect freedom'. It is not only extended at the
level at which freedom of mind and limb is already possessed by
people. It is enhanced and lifted to a more directing position by
three facts: first that a person's mental horizon is drawn outwards
from a constricting concern with self to a wider concern with an
increasing section of the 'outside' world. The trap which catches
those who care neither for God nor much for fellow man is that
their concern revolves round a shrinking centre which is self,
and thus sets in that process of which the Christian is warned, the
death of the soul which cuts itself off from love of God and neighbour. They that sow to the flesh shall of the flesh reap corruption:
for where the spirit is not nurtured, the self is flesh.

Secondly, freedom is extended by the simple fact that the person who is in a lively and practised relationship with God receives
by the Holy Spirit enlarged powers of mind (and sometimes of
limb) to do and perceive those things of which the larger horizon
gives scope and opportunity and challenge. Christ did not say
idly, 'I am come that they might have life, and have it abundantly,'
even though he implied life gained through tribulation. His
winning of the psychic and spiritual supremacy over the bondages
which the world brings on human lives is passed to his people in
the grace of the Holy Spirit who proceeds from the Father and
from the Son.

Thirdly, it is deepened because God is seen to be both the
creative power behind everything, to be in the last issue in control of whatever happens, and through Christ's supremacy to be
making all things work together for good. In the light of this
awareness, much anxiety is dissolved because dilemmas and
difficulties are not seen as ultimate disasters, and the toils and
tribulations of the world are not seen as casting doubt on God's
purpose or God's goodness. Perhaps most liberating of all is that
God is indeed Master of all that is; he is the person whose opinion
and judgment really matter, and another anxiety is reduced
concerning what other people think or judge about one's self or

one's deeds.

When all that has been said, it must at once be acknowledged that there are a very great many people whose horizons of awareness are magnificently extended towards the 'outside' world, who work with zeal and love for those who need, who are very much alive and very little concerned with self. There is an unarguable reality in the idea of the church mystical, those who do good things for God, who are indubitably pleasing to God and have their share in the attitude and the compassion of Christ, even though they do not acknowledge that participation or own to any allegiance in that direction, or even deny his very existence. God does not reject the deeds of those who, for one reason or another, cannot find it in themselves to believe in him.

Their freedom is enlarged by their love of others and their lack of anxiety about themselves. They share in the freedom of the sons of God, even though the origin of it is hidden from them. And yet it is an inescapable fact of reality that their freedom is less near to perfect freedom than is the freedom of the believer who consciously maintains contact between his own deeps and the deeps of God. It was also no idle statement when Christ said, 'I, if I be lifted up, will draw all men unto me.' Since men and women are conscious and rational beings, the potential texture of their ultimate divinity is completed only when its threads are drawn together in open recognition of divine majesty. While the believer is open to the thought, discussion, speculation and wonder which from time to time bears in upon him or her, the unbeliever is held back from free-ranging contemplation of such large matters and blocked from perception of them by unwillingness to recognize them should they come near. But the gaps and the blockages are ones which will (surely) the most easily vanish, since already the whole character of the personality is, though unconsciously, impregnated with that quality of which God's own nature consists.

ᴄ 10 ᴐ

Pain Under Challenge

PAIN IS FAR from being anyone's favourite subject. If love is
the most desired among human experiences, then pain is certainly
the most dreaded. In talking about it, it must be remembered that
this small word describes every imaginable shade and variation of
physical suffering and of emotional anguish. It is a universal
reality throughout the animal world. No creature of flesh and
blood is without it. For all we are able to know, it may exist in
the realm of plant life also. It is possible that in the lower animals
physical pain predominates. But in the human make-up, psychic-
ally more developed and complex, there is an enormous area of
vulnerabilities of heart and mind. Each man and woman is open
to the discovery of private heavens and of private hells, the latter
in pains of body and in hidden pains of feeling.

Most dreaded and disliked it certainly is, yet this piece of evolutionary equipment is for mankind the most vital in all his armoury.
If it could be abolished, it would have to be invented again
immediately, for it occupies a truly astonishing place in the unfolding of the creation scheme. Evolution tells us of the necessity
of pain in the business of biological development. At the same
time it is a central raw material for man's entry into that dimension
of love which lies beyond evolution. It is indispensable for the
survival and progress of the humblest species, yet it is the experience most deeply shared between God and man, and helps to
bring man towards that love which characterizes him in his
intended divine likeness. For love in any dimension which might
be called divine is inseparable from the fact and the experience of
suffering.

It is an enduring thread running through the whole human story from its most primitive animal background to its most profound spiritual experience. This earthy equipment of evolutionary survival becomes, in man, a kind of assault course through which man is challenged to discover deeper meanings of love and more selfless expressions of it. Provided out of the evolutionary cradle, it becomes paradoxically a principal mechanism by which the human spirit perceives its place in a hierarchy transcending evolution. For man standing at the end of his long evolutionary journey and now at the threshold of a further dimension of being, pain holds a position of crucial importance.

It is more the business of the biologist than of the theological thinker to detail the various functions and importances which pain fulfils in evolutionary processes. No doubt he would say that the whole of evolution and the very existence and survival of living species would be unimaginable without it. It is not hard for the uninformed layman to see that all the positive needs and satisfactions of life are backed by an ultimate sanction of pain and that to the satisfying of such needs as hunger, thirst, sex, rest or warmth are given their urgency by the pains which quickly follow if these things are denied. It is equally easy to understand that pain is the natural warning of damage threatened or done, and that in all sorts of ways behaviour is dictated by the messages which pain conveys.

The theological thinker, on the other hand, has the infinitely engrossing task of working out what part is played by pain in the economy of the creation and how it may hinder or assist man in his progress to spiritual awareness. More people than might admit to the fact would like to be able to look out on the world and to feel confident that they belong to a system with a purpose and with a recognizably positive outcome. But for many of them the array of human sufferings confronting them is a bar to such confidence and appears as a cogent argument (and sometimes a convenient excuse) for dismissing any belief in a good God and in a purposeful creation. And unless the theological thinker can expose the position of crucial importance which pain holds and make its existence in God's world comprehensible, these people, lacking this confidence, will not believe.

There is no conclusion to be arrived at save that God will not and cannot withdraw pain from his creation. It is irrevocably connected with the act of creating and with the exercise of love. The glimpse of the Lamb 'slain before the foundation of the world' states this truth, and the Christ within creation acts it out with irrevocable certainty. Our own observations confirm it when we set about some small creating, or when we see some barrier of pain which must be passed in the doing of an action of selfless love. It is inescapably evident that pain is present not by divine permission only but in some strange way by divine necessity also. It is the unavoidable condition of a world where love is the end-fulfilment and where freedom is the means of its development.

The scientist, the humanist or the idealist of any philosophy may dream sometimes of doing away with suffering and of releasing mankind from pain. But pain will not be done away. Try to banish it and it springs up again some other way. Escape it, and all you do is to leave it for someone else to bear. Salve it in revenge and you throw it back to breed and proliferate – and to touch you and others afresh. Drug it or drown it and you get side-effects or hangovers. Let technology bring out its wonders of skill and invention and every one benefits in some way; but utopia does not come. Pain simply shifts its ground and you get pollution, poverty, stress diseases, inflation and industrial discontents. The strange paradox about pain, seen in its widest context, not just as physical or 'medical' pain but as the painfulness throughout human relationships, is that it takes the confronting and experiencing of pain to accomplish the healing of pain. All the devices of mankind for his progress and his comfort are good and useful. But they do not assuage his pain, for his pain is not mainly bodily discomfort. The facing of pain can bring healing because in the facing of pain there is concealed the exercise of love. The skills and devices of man confer their benefits at a certain level of well-being. But ultimately only love heals. Perhaps one of the most important discoveries that any person can make is that all the instant panaceas to which our evolutionary natures cling and on which they depend are bought with a high price of pain and have no lasting power to emancipate; and that the only lasting panacea which has no side-effects is God.

It might seem strange to say that pain, and not love, is the most significant of human experiences. But this brings out a fact of great importance and helps to clear up a long-standing confusion. It enables us to see the dramatic process of development in which love has appeared and begun to win its way amid the hazards and ruggednesses of the creative process.

Evolution has opened up to us the idea of a developing, unfolding creation in which everything comes, and has come, by slow stages and in which nothing arrives or has arrived ready-made. There is an order of events, an emergence of new elements and new situations; there are new tensions and juxtapositions, increasing evidences of harmony and of purpose. To use a modern expression, the creation has to be regarded as a dynamic process, not as a static state. This radically alters our outlook.

In the traditional days gone by when the Garden of Eden stories were still the basis of all Christian thinking about man's origin (and were indeed the only account to which thinking man could look) there was no alternative to believing that the human race came ready-made into existence with Adam and Eve, endowed from the beginning (as befitted man in God's image) with instant love, goodness and spiritual awareness. Upon this pristine perfection, so it had to be supposed, pain and death stole in, dark strangers which would not have come but for the consequences of man's disobedience. This set of ideas, which has held the floor right through the Christian era, told of paradise given and paradise lost, of love first possessed and love (almost) lost, of man in favour and man fallen from favour. Ultimately it told of paradise regained, of love restored and man reprieved. But all the same it made it very difficult to understand the seemingly hopeless jumble of good and evil, love and hate, sin and virtue with which the world is filled. And it posed severe problems in the working out of how Christ's sufferings brought about a solution to the strange entanglement.

The reality provided by evolution (and palaeontology) is strikingly different. The dynamic view of creation allows these difficult problems to fall into place. Nothing has in fact come ready-made into this world; neither Adam, nor love, nor goodness, nor spiritual awareness. Not even Christ came full-formed, but was born of woman and was perfected in suffering. A process of growing and becoming characterizes everything which God creates and even which God begets: '. . . first the blade and then the ear then the full corn in the ear.'

It was not like that at all; it was the other way about. It was not love which came first but pain. Pain was the original possession, the first companion of life, the mainspring of its forward movement. Pain is incomparably more ancient than love, the most ancient, probably, of all biological experiences. For us evolutionary creatures pain has long been a fully operative mechanism, its existence stretching back down the long corridor of our advance to humanity. It has been, for us too, the necessary companion from the beginning, the central nerve of our evolutionary equipment.

Love is a far more recent comer into our existence. It is the herald of the new dimension of the human spirit, the proof of man's unique status among all other life forms. In days as relatively recent as his earthly life, Christ had to talk of love as the new commandment! Religious insight and most particularly the hard-won spiritual realization of the Old Testament had only begun to point towards it. But love was not only a latecomer in the human story; it was also a very slow one. Pain comes unbidden, and requires no patient striving for its experiencing. Love that may be truly called love must be sought and striven for in self-givings and self-sacrifices, through efforts and often against natural reluctances. At its most exacting apex it is perfected in forgiveness (not only divine but also human), where love continues undeflected by painfulness of body or of mind.

Pain was already ancient beyond compare before the first flickering light of love dawned upon the human horizon. With that dawning, man at long last stepped out beyond the logic of evolution. By that light (albeit only flickering) he was beckoned towards a dimension of spirit of which evolution could not have dreamed and which, even more certainly, the forces of evolution could never bring to completion. Round this relationship between man's two most significant experiences – pain, the enduring groundwork of life, and love, the new dimension arising out of it – was to revolve the whole subsequent drama of man's spiritual history.

Love, the capacity which (after intellect) was finally and decisively to separate man from all his relations in the animal world and to set his course towards the struggle for spirituality and divine kinship, must have trembled as a newcomer amid the entrenched power of the natural evolutionary processes. It still trembles and often hides itself from the pains encountered in the pursuit of truth, justice, righteousness and forgiveness. The very nature of love's perfection was shown to be that which will not hide nor defend itself in the accomplishment of what that present requires. At the same time the evolutionary equipments in nature, with their defences, aggressions and competitions, ride roughshod over the demands of love and bring massive persuasions to bear against its demands. They ridicule it and often crucify it. Yet love is destined under God to be the greatest thing of all, stretching untouched through the death of the natural evolutionary self as the principal of that which is eternal. Tender plant it may be in a sense, but it is no hot-house growth, for it must gain a supremacy amid all the robustness and ruggedness of man's evolutionary powers and driving forces. It must itself be robust and rugged, at once fearless and selfless. In Christ it was all these things, and the robustness and the ruggedness meant the power to confront the evolutionary pull which binds man to his past and to his animal ancestry. And the confronting of evolutionary pull means the challenging of the pain which is the mainspring of all the evolutionary mechanism. The whole of man's seeming unrest lies in this dramatic fact that out of evolutionary nature with all its lowly and explosive associations shall be forged the supernatural love which shall transcend evolution, sublimating its equipments and sweeping them into the service of its ultimate divine likeness. Some of man's multiple sufferings may arise in detail out of his sinfulnesses, but in the long perspective they are the necessary product of the clash between the powerful forces of his evolutionary nature and the even more imperious demand of his inward being for an entry into that divine kinship of love without which his being is an empty evolutionary shell. The vital question is what the new power of love does with the old raw material of evolution and with the pain at its heart. It fell to the Christ to accomplish the irreversible foundations of that transcending and of that sublimating. It fell to him to stand amid that unrest and hammer out the final shape of creation: to grasp the multiple sufferings and achieve over them a supremacy of loving creativity. 'There was none other good enough. . .' says the hymn. Yes indeed; but there was none other who by divine appointment was at once the child of evolution and the man (or Man) of the divine dimension beyond evolution, who could lay himself open to every caprice and painfulness which evolution could produce and summon such will of creative love that those caprices and painfulnesses could be drawn back into the resources of the divine plan.

It might be tempting to draw a picture of love arising to confront and overcome the pain which was indigenous to the evolutionary processes. It might be cast in the role of man's enlightenment striving to tame the roughness of his primitive background and cast out the pains which were man's enemy. It would make a neat little denouement, but it would be a complete misunderstanding of the real and dramatic depth of the situation. It might

be some part of a humanist philosophy, but it would miss the point
of Christianity which has the juxtaposition of love and pain at its
centre. It would be a passport for pessimism, since the pain is still
prolific and unrest so rife.

The task of love, the newcomer on the evolutionary scene, was
to confront the raw materials of man's nature and the painfulnesses
of his evolutionary background and to insist that they should be
the vehicles of his forthcoming kinship with the divinity of the
Creator. It was not ordained to promote human well-being and
comfort in a worldly sense but to begin to produce man's divinity
out of the earthy elements of his flesh and blood. It was not there
only to banish or suppress pain but to take hold of the impulses and
occasions of pain and turn them to divine account. It was there to
draw man's complex evolutionary responses into the simple yet
exacting channel of response to God's grace.

Christianity does not see pain as the enemy. It was dreaded and
disliked, certainly, but all depends upon the spirit in which the
response to pain is made. The enemy lies deeper than pain and
behind it, the impulse which would use pain to provoke, to deter
man from good and to deflect him from the divine kinship which is
his ultimate and complete fulfilment. There is a response also of
love which will quell the provocations and angers raised by pain,
which will face pain for the sake of goodness, and which will
cement the spirit of man more closely to the spirit of God because
of pain. The thing in which love becomes most powerful and most
clearly intertwined with pain is forgiveness, where love triumphs
completely over the provocations offered by pain and in which the
spirit of man is brought closest of all to the Spirit of God. Pain is
not the enemy, because while it can destroy and lead to evil, it
can exalt and lead to God.

❧ 11 ❧

Pain Exploited

IF PAIN IS one of the main and most original necessities of life and companion of experiment and all its advances, then its presence is fundamentally good and creative, for life and its processes are the Creator's and evolution is the unfolding of his purpose. Had this world been some utopian place in which nothing went wrong, the amount of pain might have been exactly tailored to the requirements of the biological situation – growing pains on the largest scale. But there is no utopian perfection here and nothing is either ready-made or tailor-made. Instead there is freedom, in which mankind was destined to arise and to make the dramatic transition from creature of evolution to a status higher than angels, sharing kinship with God; a transition which God not only ordained but in the forging of which he himself took part. This freedom is freedom in the truest sense and of the most rugged, lofty and exacting nature, for in it the creature of evolution has to form the embryo of his divinity, meeting the challenges and the sufferings which freedom presents and learning ultimately the mysteries of love and the painfulnesses of love. Thus he deepens character in the brush and touch with hazards and caprices, and, if he is fortunate enough, comes to perceive his need of God's grace, which alone brings divinity to evolution and draws the hazards and the sufferings into possibilities of creativeness.

In this freedom a strange mystery of evil exists: yet not altogether a mystery, because freedom is large enough and God's plan is sure enough to contain opposition not only in the mean little rebellions of man's imagination but in the more powerful and sinister regions of the spirit. The existence of the power whom

Christ called Satan (and who is known in many parts of the East as the Satan or Shaitan) is also not wholly surprising if we consider that man, on his journey towards his divinity, must encounter every possible hazard and caprice, every possible barrier and enmity between him and his surpassing prize. (Here the divine ecology again peeps through, since freedom has its price of hazard and the goal which freedom makes possible is reached only by way of passing through the hazard which freedom produces!) Were it not for the opposition of such an enemy, mankind would not be constrained to seek the grace of God and would therefore not know of his intended participation in divine nature. Of such a situation without either divine government or malign opposition in spiritual places the humanist interpretation of life consists. It is presumably possible that it may be true: the entire story of religion, and particularly of Christian belief, may be a wild surmise. However, the interpretation of the pains and hazards of existence, as provided by the religious experiences of Christianity and by the scientific knowledge of evolution taken together, appear to give a panorama of incomparably greater depth of focus and width of perspective. Such an interpretation takes the divine nature of God as real, the demonic intelligence of Satan as real, the incarnation of Christ as real and man's destiny of relationship with God resulting from Christ's incarnation as real. These realities are the background to the present discussion.

In the freedom which the divine scheme envisages for man's journey through evolution, the spirit of evil was given liberty to operate, to tempt, to corrupt and to destroy. (If freedom is truly freedom so that evil is permitted, evil itself is truly evil, and is not play-acting but in earnest in the part of opposition.) It has already been suggested that pain is the piece of evolutionary equipment which the demon long ago chose as his weapon with which to dominate man's conduct and destroy man's aspiration for divine kinship. It was, in a colloquial sense, an absolute gift, because pain backed by the urges of desire and need is the basic galvanizer to action and provoker of reaction. In a more literal sense, it was in truth freedom's gift to the power of evil, yet a gift permitted by the Creator because in it lay the secret of the ultimate grandeur of man's spirit.

If pain was already ancient and established long before love began to appear, evil was also ancient and was in the process of establishing its hold upon the human scene. Pain, the natural spur to action of the evolutionary world, was beginning to serve evil's purpose as a means of provoking aggressions more important than the simple aggressivenesses and defensivenesses of animal instinct. These were not just acts damaging the body and soon forgotten, but were angers and enmities wounding the soul and often long remembered. The demon could not exactly take pain as his own possession, but he could make it his own preserve where he developed his technique and perfected his skill. He had the freedom of those heartlands of the human personality where vulnerability lies and where provocability is ever present. For a long time he had no challenger, for that challenger was the latecomer on the scene called love, which had a long and painful struggle ahead to gain even the beginnings of acceptance, let alone supremacy.

The demon had no more to do than to accentuate the fear of pain, the suspicion of danger, the threat of enmity. Pain in its multiple forms could be a wholly reliable means of dictating human reactions. As man became more sensitive and more self-conscious, the areas of his vulnerability became more extensive, and from fearing the hurt of the body he soon came to fear hurt to the mind.

The power, whatever it or he may be, to whom Christ referred as the prince of this world planted himself in the midst of the evolutionary process, not in the animal world but in the part of it where man was getting ready to enter the experience of love and to fulfil his destiny of divine kingship. By usurping for his own use the command of pain, he concealed himself at the fountainhead of human reaction and took possession of the roots of human conduct. By manipulation of the natural desire for advantage and the natural fear of pain he was strategically placed to deflect the will from good and to tip it in the direction of evil, to set one man's hand against another and one man's heart against his neighbour. By playing on the fear of the unknown and of the loss of freedom of will he could make the idea of God unimportant or even abhorrent because self was of such all-consuming importance. With this weapon he was able to become as a strong man armed, keeping his possession of man's reactions by maintaining the dreads surrounding pain. And with man's developing sensitivities not of body but of feeling, pride and selfhood, the extent of his vulnerabilities increased, where pain might provoke and provocations cause pain.

It is important to take note of this proposition that by choosing, and establishing a proprietory control over, this instrument of pain, the power of evil succeeded in establishing his presence at the centre of evolutionary processes and in the heartlands of human personality. When later, after a long apprenticeship in ordinary human beings, the divine love was to come to confront evil power, pain was to be the chosen ground for that confrontation, and the power of love was to make its bid to establish its own sovereignty (ejecting the usurper) within the heartlands and over the dreads surrounding the experience of pain. In the gaining of this sovereignty or supremacy, divine love was to translate the whole evolutionary product of humanity, from the heart and outwards, into the new language of the divine dimension beyond evolution. As yet (and even more so before Christ) evil has the freedom of the heartlands and still controls the products of evolutionary heritage ('the whole world lies in the evil one'). Yet the heart is to be the place of origin of the kingdom of heaven, and human make-up the framework for eternal life. In Christ, who was essentially man of evolution and man of the dimension beyond evolution, there was destined to be formed from the raw materials of evolutionary make-up shared with humanity a style of personality wholly transcending the evolutionary model, and sharing with God the qualities of the divine dimension. The principle of what Christian religion has called resurrection (and other long words like redemption) is the exchanging, at the centre of personality, of the controlling power of evil for the controlling power of love, over those vulnerabilities to pain which are the roots of conduct. It is not hard to detect (even in this threshold land of our present dispensation) in the response to opposition, criticism or adversity, the mark of someone in whose demesne the embryo of the divine dimension has begun to establish a supremacy at these roots of personality. In Christ, the first of men in whom the dimension beyond evolution was seen, this translation was an original act of new creation between God and Christ. In man, the many of whom Christ was first, the metamorphosis is by the grace, the new creative stream, coming from that act of new creation. For man in his lifetime here, the exchanging of the sovereignty of evil for the sovereignty of love is the whole of his spiritual pilgrimage; and its accomplishment, to be known in full only after this dispensation, is the finishing of the new creation of man made complete in God and God made complete in man. And since we are never to be allowed to let reality become unreal or ideas of divinity become too divine, we are to see God and ourselves bearing the scars and showing the marks of the pains of that long evolutionary pilgrimage which gave to God his creation and to the creation, by grace, its divinity.

This evil power concealed behind the outward facade of our existence held and still holds his deadly hatred of man because of this high destiny for which man is marked out. Could he but hold this position unconquered, he might continue to confuse men and women about the meaning of their pain-ridden situation and hold them back from their destiny by deceiving them into thinking that their best interest was in self-protection and self-interest, aggressiveness and the revenge which gets its own back. Thus he might keep man's nose to the grindstone of pain, self-defence and sin. He exercised his enmity against man by sowing enmity between men. Angers and hatreds, greeds and meannesses took their part in everyone's lives and people got hurt right, left and centre. Quite apart from strange natural disasters and incomprehensible diseases, people inflict pain on one another all the time, husbands on wives, wives on husbands, parents on children, children on parents. No doubt the sins of the fathers and of the children went on (and go on) far beyond the third and fourth generation. Of the supremacy of evil and the proliferation of his devices it seemed that there would be no end, and the human horizon was filled with anxiety and the prospect of pain. People could be excused in time past, as they may be excused now, for thinking that pain and evil are indivisible, that pain simply is evil and that evil simply is to suffer. Here lies what is probably the greatest mystification of all and greatest cause of indignation and disbelief concerning the Christian faith for the people of today. After Christ and after 2,000 years of Christianity pain is not only (so it is thought) not diminished but seen actually to be increased and the world (seemingly) in greater disarray than ever. But the advent of love and the coming of Christ was not simply (as has been said before) to mollify pain but rather to defeat the evil which made of pain a proliferating horror. That is to say, while alleviating pain and making life more bearable at every opportunity, the task is to discern in pain some unseen potentiality for good and to disallow to pain every potentiality for the provocation of evil.

It may well have seemed that suffering is the dominant evil of the world, provoking and destroying. Yet nevertheless it has not lost its creative capacity. Despite the fact that it has become so inextricably entangled with evil, the fundamental creativity belonging to pain had not disappeared. It cannot be anything but unpleasant and dreaded, and yet nature observes it as part of its necessary equipment; and, as has been suggested, if it could be abolished it would have to be invented again. It accompanies much of creative effort and acts as a spur to nature's progresses. Teilhard de Chardin, in *The Phenomenon of Man*, pointed out that every major advance in evolution has been achieved at the cost of prodigious effort and prodigious pain. It has lain behind life's advance and behind the establishment of nature's ecologies. It is (alongside of necessity) the father of invention and it imparts strength to survive in persecution or adversity. Its impact has made the wisdom of law-making possible, and from its cause and effect the concept of words arose. Above all it must have been a progenitor of love, urging protectiveness and calling forth compassion (and ultimately giving birth to the idea of sacrifice and substance to the meaning of forgiveness). Pain may be overwhelmingly the preserve and the plaything of evil, the enemy and the destroyer, but it is also the thing required by God in creation, capable of being ally and creator, even though, to our frail feelings, unwelcome ally and unwelcome creator.

It was to be a long time, as we may surmise looking back down our evolutionary story, before pain was to take a part in the spiritual life of humanity and become a creative factor there too. But when love began to dawn in human consciousness, mankind was set on a new course and his destiny of relationship with the creator came distantly into view. There began to grow (and this is one of the main significances of the Old Testament) the perception of love as the basis of right relationship, of sacrifice as an expression of worship and the understanding that pain had some mysterious part to play in man's developing relationship with God. Then there came (and this is the main significance of the New Testament) the declaration in the words and acts of Christ that the over-riding requirement of love is that it shall shun none of the pains of man's freedom or man's wickedness but meet them in the power which love gives, drawing them into a relation again with the creative purpose of God, and in so doing make forgiveness possible.

Out of all this there emerges a truth of rather startling significance. It is that pain, in itself, is neutral. It can belong in the camp of God's creativeness or in the camp of evil's destructiveness. It is simply a part of evolutionary equipment, ancient and omnipresent. It takes its moral colouring not because of what it is in itself but from the spirit which lies behind what it is made to do and what is done with it. The action concerned with it shifts from the phenomenon of pain itself to the deeper forces which contend for control of it; for it is, as we have seen, the centre of a web, of an empire, almost indeed of creation. Who gains the centre of that vital communication system gains the soul and spirit of man.

The author of a book about the war in South-East Asia used this same word about the jungle in which much of the fighting took place. The jungle, he said, was neutral. It favoured neither side. It was simply there, ancient and omnipresent, the permanent surroundings in which each side lived and ate and slept and in which the battle was conducted. The jungle itself could be a foe if one allowed it to be, sapping energy, obsessing the mind, driving to desperation. But it could also be turned into an ally if one learned its ways. The real action was directed against the far more cunning enemy who lurked under its cover and used it to carry out his stratagems.

Pain, like the jungle, is neutral. This fact has consequences of startling importance. Nothing has brought so much confusion as the idea that pain, omnipresent, recurring and inextinguishable, is evil. For if this were truly so, there would be no answer to the question 'How does God allow this in his creation?' It would be (and for many people is) a door wide open to pessimism and despair because there is no wholesale cure for it, no painless Utopia around the corner, no prospect of its eradication. This also casts a veil of obscurity over the interpretation of the crucifixion.

So soon, on the other hand, as we may grasp the essential neutrality of the actual fact of pain and see it, like the jungle, as the battle-ground not the battle, then it becomes possible to see that in the battle-ground of the experiencing of pain it is possible for evil to be put down and for love, in the same experiencing, to be brought to its most authentic expression. Over the issue of pain a far more important issue than pain has to be decided; a far more cunning and powerful enemy has to be defeated. Over that issue in the long apprenticeships of religion man tried and failed and tried and failed in moral obedience. (Have I the power to set my face to a way of self-sacrifice and to scorn the line of least resistance? The answer was never completely 'yes'.) But eventually over the same issue love grown to maturity came to its encounter in full depth with pain and by it to confrontation with the evil lurking behind pain and using it for its strategies. In Christ half-seen questions and half-realized principles came openly to the fore. To whom shall pain belong and whose influence shall gain the supremacy when pain threatens? Who shall rule the responses of those vulnerable heartlands which evolution has provided but which the creature plan claims as raw material of heaven? Shall evil be returned for evil and revenge for revenge, or shall love be returned in exchange for evil and forgiveness in return for pain? To whom shall the roots of action and springs of conduct respond?

Christian thought has interpreted Christ's crucifixion almost exclusively as being God's provision for man's forgiveness. That this is the epicentral truth of religion there can be no doubting. This was clearly expressed by Christ and is the culmination of the whole of the Old Testament history and of the best level of Old Testament insight. (It is not unremarkable that an explanation of man's spiritual destiny made from the point of view of evolution leads inexorably to the conclusion that forgiveness holds the key to the unravelling of the whole problem.) Nevertheless Christian thought has had almost insoluble problems in explaining how it is that the suffering of Christ has accomplished man's forgiveness. It will be easier to understand what the inner action of forgiveness really is if we look at it as an encounter with pain in which love gains the supremacy and evil has no opportunity to proliferate. Forgiveness is the exact reverse of rendering evil for evil under the stress of pain. It is the rendering of unbroken and uninterrupted love in return for whatever pain of malice or injustice has been inflicted. But it has to be understood that to give back only love for hurt is extremely far from acting weakly as a doormat on which others may tread with impunity. The moral demand that lies upon the forgiven is as powerful as the moral requirement of the forgiver to forgive. Christ holds the world in his claim upon it to match love with love, and the world can only be at peace with itself (and with him) when this claim has been met.

Christian thought has emphasized the forgiveness of man by God. It has failed to give enough emphasis to the forgiving of one person by another. (When the word forgiveness is used, that ordinary person to whom this book is addressed will think almost automatically of our forgiveness by God – and will quail a little inwardly.) But what arises as the consequence of Christ's action is the part which we humans must play in this great endeavour. We have not solely to look to our own forgiveness from God. As Christ said clearly (though it is not recorded frequently), we have to achieve a great extent of forgiving of one another because only in that way do we begin to carry into practice what Christ accomplished in principle. His confrontation with pain and his winning of supremacy of love within pain constitute forgiveness, and they also make the cutting edge of the defeat of evil.

From Christ's work there proceeds the grace enabling us to carry that word forward; and from our forgiveness is the claim demanding that we should do so. Here in this arena of our freedom the defeat of evil is being carried on. That cutting edge is given from his hands into ours. It is in us that love is now destined to strive for supremacy within the experience of pain. In us the drama of divine purpose continues its unfolding and its new creating. While the defeat of evil is being brought to realization here (for as evil more and more betrays itself, so love more and more is challenged to rise against it), other things are happening in the working of the divine ecology. The pain which was seen as being part of nature's equipments of advance is now to be detected as part of the mechanism of supernatural advance. And our meeting of pain, our overcoming of it by grace known or unknown, our forgivenesses and the victories of love in spite of hurt, are the things which pre-eminently build us up in the likeness of God and advance us a little more on our own threshold of love. Pain is an anvil on which many principal spiritual issues are hammered out and qualities forged. If that meeting of suffering with love which denotes forgiveness was the experience in which Christ 'was made perfect in suffering', then that must also be the way of our own perfection and the means of our first touches of participation in divine nature.

ও 12 ৬

Pain the Stronger Man's Armour

IF WE LOOK BACK over the ground already covered, what we may begin to see emerging is a story of creation in which the presence of pain has a surprisingly, even disconcertingly, constant and central significance.

Pain existed originally for the purpose of protecting life and for the sake of the evolution to which life was committed. It was the important, uncomfortable, natural equipment by which life was spurred to adapt to new circumstances and to progress in more complex techniques of survival. Indeed were it not uncomfortable it would not be important; for the fear of pain is the beginning of self-protection.

Being already present as a part of evolutionary make-up (and this is the really striking thing which we can now see if we come to terms with the fact of our evolutionary background), it stood ready to become part of a profounder equipment in the spiritual order of things as man ventured out towards the threshold of his relationship with God. Having acted at a humble level amid the ascent of evolution, it was to fulfil a higher function in the quest for spirit and in the discovery of love. It was to be not less uncomfortable but more poignantly so, for the quest and the reward of discovery were of incomparably greater worth. How may we know that this is not just fanciful surmise? How may we convince ourselves that pain is not, after all, simply the alien, the enemy which must be rooted out by technical skills? We can tell the validity of this argument by the way in which the rather strange pieces of the jigsaw puzzle fit together to make a picture, leaving no stray pieces for which places cannot be found. If we grasp first of all the 'secular' necessity of pain and its universal presence throughout man's evolutionary ancestry, and then see its invasion of the psychic and spiritual experience of men and women, we may be led to the realization that it is not only there, an ontological fact of life, but that it is there possessing an essential significance. Then if we look at the coming of Christ, we see something which makes absolute sense against this background of our unceasing unrest. We see Christ confronting pain, seizing the initiative in the handling of it, and within that experience establishing a supremacy of love so that pain is brought back once again to God's preserve, robbed of its ultimate enmity and made into a pathway of new creation, a crossing of the threshold. The meaning of our unrest lies in evolutionary man questing his spiritual destiny. Christ, the man of evolution (born of Mary) and man of heaven (conceived by the Holy Ghost), was penetrating the reality of our unrest and translating it wholly into creativity. In the quest of spirit the high peak of meaning is reached where two seeming opposites meet in juxtaposition – pain the legacy of evolution and love the dynamic of the new dimension. There all the threads come together and the purpose of the human odyssey – painful and beautiful – has its unfolding. The raw materials of evolution are finally converted into the completeness of divine nature, and the enmity within evolution is shown to be ultimately and in the last issue conquerable.

As mankind has pulled away from his evolutionary background he finds ever more clearly that pain has not been providentially withdrawn, nor has he been able, for all his technical achievements, to vanquish it. Rather, indeed, the opposite is true. Leaping forward to discover new horizons of knowledge and tasting new experiences of mind and spirit, he has nevertheless found himself surrounded more insistently by pain and turbulence. He does not luxuriate in less suffering but is challenged paradoxically by more. And man, idealist and comfort-lover, seeker for the good and sucker for self-interest, is mystified and disgruntled.

It is not by any divine carelessness that it is there, nor is it simply a consequence of man's wickedness, although man's wickedness does most frequently increase its incidence. It is there by a strange and profound necessity in the total economy of the providence in which man is to be formed in the image of God. It does not provide any argument against God – and if it did, should we be better off? The pain of the world would remain and we should be left to struggle with it unaided. It does provide something other than argument and something very different. Besides all its secular necessities, it remains as the only anvil we know on which love is hammered out, and the only yardstick we have by which love may be measured. For how else may we know the power of love save by the hell and high water through which it is prepared to go, and what else more instantly brings love to the fore than the pain or the danger of one whom we must recognize as a fellow human being? The painfulnesses without which life and the preservation of species would have been un-thinkable seem to be the pain without which, in man, love and the hankering for God might well have never been possible to fulfil.

Before the denouement of the tangled plot of evolution and divinity, pain and love, began to dawn, a long process of creation had to take its course. The millennia of prehistory – in which in-deed a thousand years or a million were but as a day – saw the arrival and the disappearance of plants and animals, and out of the evolutionary boiling-pot eventually man arose. But now, as every good fairy story tells (and fairy stories are often parables of truth about real life), things had to 'go wrong' before they could come right, and defeat had to be risked before victory could be won. In the freedom of the divine enterprise evil was (and is) permitted to exist and to make its bid to sabotage the divine plan and to destroy up-and-coming man. Pain (that uncomfortable piece of life's equipment) was the ideal agent by which his action might be influenced and dominated, the back door through which a foot-ing could be gained on human motive and thought, and the occupation of the heartlands of personality undertaken. Pain is everywhere, and the instinct of survival is at the centre of every person, and so everywhere evil could spread its tentacles by touching the ancient instincts of defence and aggression. The whole world lay entangled in self-interest and, most subtle weapon of all evil's ingenuity, love which strove to overcome evil is more vulnerable than all else. For the devil to make the way of love seem most painful of all – which indeed it is – was the winning card by which he held his own supremacy.

One can see how deep this strategy of evil was. The threat of pain was the whiplash by which man was held in the power of evil; love was the power which should challenge evil; but love was itself the most vulnerable to pain!

Indeed as men and women rode roughshod over one another's needs and sensitivities, none could wholly undo the instinctive reaction for self-fulfilment and self-protection, none could counter the power of threatened self-interest. Love, privately seen or publicly codified in religious precept, kept men and women sometimes from the grossest acts of violence and selfishness, but in smaller things they would not, could not, face the minor painfulnesses of selflessness. Human love could do something, but not enough; it could go some distance in special relationships, but not far enough. For love was not only not yet fully known, but it proceeds from where evil had established its prior and stronger hold.

Returning to the image of the fairy story, none could overcome the enemy until such time as the prince, the son of the king, was ready to challenge evil at the point of stronghold from which his weapons dominated mankind's countryside. That stronghold was the heart of man and the weapon was pain, the dread of it, the threat of it, the prospect of it. He alone, the prince, could make the confrontation and throw out the challenge. Only he had the spiritual strength, and only he was heart-free to do it, since in his heart – unlike each human heart – evil had no footing, no answering alliance. Therefore when the onslaught of pain came, he could reply in the spirit and terminology of love. And the spirit and terminology of love in face of pain, with no answering echo of revenge, is what we call forgiveness. And forgiveness is the strong, if unspectacular, key to the defeat of evil. For it is the undoing of that paradox where the love which is evil's defeat is the apex of the pain by which evil maintains its hold. Christ came to take issue with pain so that it should no longer be a weapon in evil's armoury. With evil behind it the experience of pain can be the cause and provocation of evil; it is generally the result of evil; it is therefore the fuse which sets alight the Catherine wheel whose sparks enkindle more evil still. Evil relies apparently on this effect of pain to deflect from good and lure towards evil. If evil lost the ability to steer man's will through the threat of pain, it would lose its hold upon humanity and would lose its power to deflect humanity away from the love-relationship with God. To love God or neighbour is to lay the heartlands open to all kinds of risk of pain; and risk of pain is where the devil strikes.

It might look as if a picture were being painted of an unrelieved gloom where pain is the norm and where evil dominates the scene. It is true that St John said 'the whole world lies in the evil one', and it is true that at the touch of provocation human nature reacts (even now) more readily by way of self-defence than by way of self-sacrifice – anger is a thousand times easier than patience or forgiveness. But for the moment we are dealing with the question of pain and of its connection with evil. We have not yet come to the long-awaited question of love, long-awaited, because it dawned upon the horizon long, long after evolution had accomplished the greater part of its marvellous and painful progress.

However, just as love had its early heralds showing light before the real rising of dawn, so the transcending of pain and the sub-limating of suffering had unmistakable heralds also. The turning of painfulnesses to positive purpose can be seen throughout the plant and animal world in natural processes which we take for granted: the putting out of strong growth after pruning, the capacity of some plants to produce strong suckers in response to root damage, the willingness of animals to face danger in defending their young, and even the mechanism by which muscles grow in response to need, wounds heal and limbs regain strength. All the more is this evident in human life. The most elementary processes of living require a limitless variation on the theme of pain from the obvious ones like birth and (sometimes) death, to the daily sweat of the brow, learning of patience, overcoming of disinclination and the doing of a thousand tiresome things for the well-being of the family, of neighbours or of self. It seems to be one of the clearest proofs of our spiritual destiny that all such multiple small painfulnesses are taken both gaily and for granted into our creative efforts. For what else beside some apprehension of the divine prompts humanity as a whole to grasp so many nettles of painfulness and strive so nobly in moral effort to bring good things from their actions? If one were to answer that it is a more down-to-earth realism which does the prompting, because one wants the best for people, then it may be said in return 'Why are people important?', And if it then be answered, 'Because quite often one loves them', is this not then indeed some apprehension of the divine?

Any kind of living requires the grasping of a lot of nettles, even living alone, because it is all too easy to 'let oneself go' if one ceases to take trouble. Where communal living is concerned, and where the good of many depends on how relationships are regulated, the problem and the nettles are multiplied. The individual has to meet more challenges to his moral fibre. Both religious and legal systems contain precepts for the regulation of behaviour. Man in modern society is faced with an increasing number of demands on his altruism and on his concern for the well-being of all. He is very far from responding rightly at every point, but, out of the turbulence of events, his stature is growing, and ever profounder lessons about human need, value and dignity are being learned.

It is not therefore in the occasional great cataclysms of natural disaster that the deepest problem of pain is to be located. It is risky to make any judgments when one has not oneself been in a disaster of flood, earthquake or typhoon and seen family and possessions swept away. But it is possible to guess that in such a situation the magnitude and the suddenness of what happens has the effect of rallying many resources of the human spirit in mutual help and comfort. Moreover there is no one to hate, no long-drawn resentment against human agency for what has happened.

The problem of pain lies more deeply in the innumerable woundings, injustices and enmities which flow back and forth from human vulnerability to human vulnerability, leaving legacies of anger, hatred, resentment and revenge. These may be smaller, less visible things, but they are the most fertile ground for the sowing of the seeds of evil. Moreover, here is the kind of area where the overcoming of pain is the most difficult and where the temptation to revenge seems to be the most over-riding. Here in the area of individual pride and need is where sin is born, grows, interacts, proliferates, warps, corrupts and bids to destroy. These are not natural disasters where men and women rise quickly to the event and a true charity is (momentarily at least) sparked off. They are the life-long hazards of being human, touching again and again sensitive areas already much wounded and waiting in anticipation of further hurt. In these things men and women rise more quickly still to the event, and sin (both momentarily and in the long term) rushes in, exacerbating, not healing, the hurt. Wherever sin lies at the door, behind it lies pain, and behind pain (it seems hard to dispute) lies the mysterious power of evil. The sole reason why evil can make such capital out of pain is that pain is the *agent provocateur* in chief, the universal fly in the ointment.

Out of all the variation of equipments and experiences given to humans it is the one which touches more points of our feeling, thinking and acting than anything else. It is therefore the one ideal instrument which the power of evil would choose with which to exert his mischief and carve out his empire.

You will not think that this is too dramatic a description if you really look at how you are influenced by the subtle pains of opening yourself to the demands of love and the pains of of being deprived of the fulfilments demanded by your own self-centredness.

Traditionally in Christianity human suffering has been painted as a mystery in some way allied to the whole problem of evil. Equally the suffering of Christ has been regarded as a mysterious, unfathomable act of divine love by which the wrong at the roots of the human situation has been reversed; and by which a limitless source of grace and forgiveness has been supplied to carry that reversal into action. In essence this reversal of evil is perfectly true, as words of Christ, of the apostles and of subsequent theology tell. Yet the hardest problem of all – for theological thinker and ordinary thinking person – was to see how the suffering of Christ really did undo the consequences of humankind's enmeshment in evil, and really did open the way to forgiveness for even the most wicked.

Perhaps it is reasonable to expect that these things should be hidden in the depths of mystery. The divine love is beyond the capacity of humans to define, and the human response to it must be in a faith which believes its efficacy without necessarily understanding its *modus operandi*. On the other hand, perhaps it is not altogether right to leave things like that; because we have received a divine promise that we shall be led into all truth – progressively deeper into the understanding of the divine ways. Moreover, ordinary thinking people, less willing now than in earlier days to accept mystery and more intent to have things made understandable, find it hard to accept the apparent fact that Christ had to go to a bloody death because there was no other way of putting things right. More difficult still, that there was no other way but this of putting right what God had apparently allowed to go wrong.

That was the kind of dilemma that awaited the thinker who probed at all deeply. The old framework of thought had no final philosophy by which to explain where the 'fault' was to be found and at whose door the world's pain must be laid. Even if (as was said all truly) there was no cause of wrong except by the sinfulness of man, this left another awkward question of responsibility. When all the cards were on the table, was it not God's error to create a humanity capable of sin, a world prone to so much suffering, people willing to perpetrate atrocities such as crucifying Christ? Mystery leaves too many questions unresolved. If the divine love is unfathomable, it is not for that reason inexplicable. By being a little more understood, its depth may be grasped as even greater and more unfathomable in goodness. And now more truth has been vouchsafed; we have been led further. And what we have been given has come from another quarter than simply religious awareness. Western Christians have, for some decades, accepted the theory of man's arrival on earth by way of the long corridor of evolution, but have not yet taken note of the flood of new light which this throws on ideas about God and man, pain, love, sin, Christ, forgiveness and the new creation. They thought the basic root of the whole matter was that of perfection spoilt by sin: and to unlock this problem they tried to take the passion of Christ and fit it straight in as a key into a lock. But it did not fit easily, as witness the generations of diverse theorizing. Something was still missing, some necessary clue, some piece in the puzzle still unfound. Christianity had to wait for the offering of science, and in the waiting time, while earlier generations pursued their quest, priceless and enduring treasures of insight were gained. Faith was deepened and the efficacy of divine grace was tested and realized.

Not that in those earlier days of knowing of the fact of evolution (and haunted still by the picture of perfection) our forebears were not in a position to lay hands on the missing piece in the picture of our problem or to spot the clue to its unravelling. They could scarcely have guessed that the clue was the seeming enemy, pain, that part of our imperfection and consequence of our fall. They did not know that pain had produced much of the quality and detail of our make-up, that it had been a driving force in our evolutionary ascent and was to play a further part in our ascent of the way of love. It was a hard thing to see that pain, which seemed so much of the problem, was actually the centre clue to the unravelling, revealing profound secrets about the grip of sin and evil and also about the liberations of love and forgiveness. But so soon as we in our day began to accept the position of pain as indigenous to the fabric of our existence, part and parcel of our make-up and at the root of every motive and action, then all the pieces in the puzzle could begin to fall into place. It is pain, lying in the hinterland of choice, emotion and action, which gives the clue to the genesis of sin, to the striving of love, and at the apex to the meaning of forgiveness and to the defeat of evil. So therefore the clue afforded by pain leads us at last logically and directly to the meaning of the encounter with pain entered – not by accident but by divine design – by Christ.

Religion is full of paradox, as for instance that in losing our life we gain it. It is a paradox too that pain and suffering, our dreaded enemies, are at the same time the means of our liberation: the problem and the solution, the puzzle and the clue. Suffering may be the good to our sinning or the power of our sacrificing, the ground of our hating or the challenge to our loving, the anvil on which is hammered out enmity or forgiveness, the point of balance from which we espouse God or the devil.

Pain has two faces; the benign face which calls out a love without measure, compassion, spiritual heroism, and the malign face which provokes and lures and multiplies pains, revenges and selfishnesses. It is as it were the root of the tree of spiritual life where God may supply the sap of creativity or the devil the sap of destructiveness. It is thus (to use a different metaphor) the hinge

on which the door of the divine purpose in man could swing this
way or that, either open for love and life and creativity, or shut,
closing the way of love and perpetuating the hold of evil over
man's body and soul.

Therefore if we ask what was happening in the passion and
crucifixion of Christ, and what was being accomplished behind
the too-familiar picture of that event and the familiar words, we
may be able to edge a little forward in our understanding and
give more confident answers. Christ was there meeting the power
of evil (the devil, the prince of this world) at the one point at
which from the outset that power had been able to dominate man's
actions. He was confronting the final weapon which evil had been
able to lay hands on to back up the desires, lusts, revenges, com-
petitivenesses and irritabilities to which human make-up is heir.
Of this final weapon he was disarming the devil by passing (as it
were) into the centre of the furnace and emerging unscathed by
all that the fire of pain might do. The lessons of his life pointed to
the truth that no strategy was of service which did not go to the
root of the problem of evil; superficial panaceas were of no interest to him, as we shall see. For him there was no alternative to a
confrontation with pain, because pain lay at the root point of the
genesis of man's deflection from good, where natural forces
belonging to the creative stream could be turned to the formation
of sin. Of the creative stream of life pain was the Achilles heel.
Lust and desire might give to the devil the first access to man's
soul, but pain provided the final and often irresistible leverage to
man's decisions.

As once he had gone to meet the maniac in Gadara armed with
nothing except the intent to love, so now he also had nothing
save a naked will and a naked body bearing the divine intent of
love. If the devil, by threat of pain, could deter the Christ from
the doing of what love required, then indeed all the kingdoms of
the world could be his. What else would there be to stand against
his sovereignty and his will for man's death and destruction? But

if the Christ could confront, pass through and overcome pain, then he would rob the devil of the ultimate power he possessed. Pain would be taken into God's preserve, into the creative stream, and the defeat of evil would be made certain. Then if this were done, there would exist the limitless supply of enabling, which we call grace, for mankind to be able to do the same, accomplish the same supremacy of love and play its part in the defeat of evil and the bringing towards completion of the sovereignty of God.

Christ went relentlessly and indeflectably to the stronghold from which the power of evil exerted pressure to make man dance to his tune. There, in a very great moral and spiritual battle, he showed it to be possible, in the summoning of every source of will, obedience and love, to emerge undeterred by these pressures. He made himself master in the hitherto demonic department of pain, drawing it back into the creative resource so that the whole structure of human personality could be freed from bondage to evolutionary forces and given the ability to grasp the life which transcends evolution. He overcame the power exerted by threat of pain to turn human action away from God and aside from the way of love. He invalidated the malign face of pain, exposing it as a threat without ultimate force. He took from evil its favourite, ancient, subtle weapon and restored it to the service of God's creativity. It is not until we have penetrated into the meaning of forgiveness that we can see the deepest point of this disarming of the devil and the most complete point at which pain is lifted to creative power. In forgiveness the love which encounters pain is made supreme, and the pain thus encountered by love is drawn finally out of the control of evil.

'When a strong man armed keepeth his palace', said Jesus, 'his goods are in peace; but when a stronger than he shall come upon him, and overcome him, he taketh from him all his armour wherein he trusted, and spoils his goods.' The devil is a strong man armed keeping hold over his human goods, and his armoury is a limitless variety of pain. Christ is the stronger, taking away the armour in which the devil trusted by matching the power of love against the force of pain, remaining undeterred until pain had spent all its resource and love had come through it to reign supreme in purpose and will.

✣ 13 ✣

Love the Intruder

LOVE WAS A latecomer in the evolutionary story; and coming long after all the other basic components of the human make-up, it was to have a function quite different from them. It is not a piece of evolutionary equipment, not an equal partner with other, and older, weapons in the evolutionary armoury. It is not evolutionary but revolutionary, an intruder and challenger upon the evolutionary scene.

It is essential to grasp this diversity of love from all else. From our everyday viewpoint it is not easy. In the business of living, there is such a multiplicity of experiences and emotions, out of which people try – if they have time to try – to make moral sense. Good and evil, hope and fear, freedom and frustration, success and failure, pain and happiness, life and death, anxiety and relief, sin and forgiveness, anger and joy and a hundred other things, all vie with each other to drag us down or to lift us up. And love; love weaves in and out of them, appearing, disappearing, given, withdrawn, sparking and dying, aspiring, being smothered – and always hankered for like the gold at the end of the rainbow. The problem, which can seem so hard, is to disentangle the priority which each possesses. They all seem to move in the same plane of existence and to be part of the same jumble, like so many weights and counter-weights on each side of some moral weighing-machine.

Yet love is not one thing among many. It is no equal partner with all the others. It is wholly distinct, and as it strengthens and is caught up into man's spiritual workings, and as it becomes accessible to the influence of grace, that difference becomes

progressively more different still. Its latecoming warns us that it
will have the quality of a stranger and pilgrim among its robust
evolutionary neighbours.

A very long time had to elapse before love made its appearance,
and in that time the evolutionary equipment of life had to establish
itself and had to lay down the necessary survival mechanisms of
pain, need, desire and fear, with thy physical responses of aggression and defence through which they were deployed. During the
ages of biological time which preceded the emergence of man,
vast by comparison with the length of human occupation of earth,
the forces of survival and progress strengthened their hold and
gained control in the deep instinctive layers of life. Evolution
pursued its unending and relentless logic of competitiveness,
self-aggrandizement and, when necessary, annihilation, while the
element of love as we know it was yet absent. In due time, in the
procreation and care of the young of more advanced species,
animal life came to contain some tiny herald of the coming dawn
of love. But, in general, in those faraway times of which we can
know little, the creative process was busy with what might be
called the first creation: the physical environment of mineral and
vegetable in which the psycho-physical complexification of animal life survived and progressed. An observer, had there been one
to observe, might have seen but slight hope of the emergence of a
life-form designated as mirroring God's nature. It is true, as we
have come lately to understand, that nature succeeds in establishing ecological balances when left to itself. Yet that harmony,
which man's violence can so easily upset, is apparently maintained by its own indigenous violence and by continual warfare.
It was out of this background that man was to emerge, within
whom that herald of love was to grow into potentiality for divine
life, and between whom and his fellows in the arena of freedom
the drama and the travail of entry into love and divine inheritance
was to take place.

Although love is not a component of the evolutionary equipment alongside others, it had to grow out of the evolutionary

processes, for there is no other way for anything to grow or to make its appearance. Nothing comes ready-made, and our evolutionary heritage contains every bit of the raw materials of our physical, mental and spiritual formation. It was evolution's work, under providence, to initiate love and to build in a foundation of the need of love, which would provide the motive power for love's development. For this it had long been preparing. But when love came, its true function began to assert itself. That strange and ultimately revolutionary function was to challenge all the deep-laid responses and devices of our evolutionary heritage and in many ways to turn topsy-turvy, inside out and upside-down, that very evolutionary equipment out of which it had first originated and which had been man's whole security. One had only to compare the natural instincts centred on self-defence with the injunction to love our enemies, to bless those who curse us and to do good to those who despitefully use us, to catch a glimpse of the distance that evolutionary man has to travel and the revolution that has to take place in him, in his entering upon the beginnings of spiritual maturity in love. The travail that that journey involves and the meetings with pain which accompany it explain a thousand things concerning mankind's apparent selfishness, his reluctance to be confronted with the reality of God and his rationalizations in side-stepping spiritual issues. It is a gulf which he is terrified to cross and against which all his evolutionary instincts rebel. The irony of the situation is that man's universal hankering for love and his destiny to possess it in divine proportion can be fulfilled only in meeting these issues and facing this demand and setting himself to cross this gulf. In turning from the travails and pains of which it holds threat, he turns from the means of his fulfilment as well as from the means of overcoming, ultimately, the sharpness of those travails and pains themselves. Here lies the focus of the radical disaffection of the world from God and of the clash that must persist within evolutionary man (or, as theology calls him, natural man), when God draws him and beckons him to venture out on his spiritual destiny. The love which brings man to the fringes of divine kinship is not the love residing in emotion or inclination. It is one in which the reconciliation with pain is an essential ingredient, and which must grow to be undeterred by the threat or prospect of suffering in the accomplishment of its purpose.

In particular, therefore, it was going to be the task of love to confront the experience of pain, to turn it also upside-down, to eject it from its commanding position at the heart of man's motive; capture its resources and bring them over into the creative armoury of God; to take that face of pain which is life-inhibiting and make it life-enhancing. In religious terminology this is summed up in the word 'redeem'. But it is theology's business to abandon names with their mystiques and to get to the work of giving existential explanations of what we now see those names to signify. Love's task is to make a confrontation with all the worst that evil can do through pain, so that, when the worst has been overcome, there is nothing worse that can ever come again. Love's task is to abandon self-defence and go to meet pain and provocation and, despite their impact, to remain unchanged, undiminished and undeterred. Love's task is to confront what keeps another in pain or bondage and, by boldness and conquest, to release the prisoner from the powers that afflict him. Love's task is ultimately to confront the source of evil and overcome the terror of his weapon of pain. It was only when Christ had come and had, in his will, act and intent, made the uncreated love of God an indigenous part of the createdness of humanity, that that confrontation could take place. As lightning he had seen Satan fall from heaven, because it is among created men that his desire and his opportunity lay. As prince of this world he came to meet the contestant of his claim to all its kingdoms. As strategist of evil he made pain his battlefield. But his opponent had long before chosen that same battlefield when, in the wilderness, he refused every other enticement. The Son of Man perceived that so long as pain was unconquered, the demon could, at a moment's notice, bend man's conduct to his will and so maintain the sovereignty

over him. Christ came to the confrontation armed with the will to
love unchangeably; the devil came armed with an impossible
weight of pain in the bid to break the will to love. If he could do
this, he would possess the souls of men for ever and hell would
have dominion. If he could not, then it was his own power that
would be broken and love would reign, and the kingdom of God
would be made certain. It is no wonder if the angels averted their
eyes at such a confrontation. Satan had power over all the evolutionary equipment: only over love could he never prevail.

Love is many things and exists at many levels, though it is always
that which is akin to the nature of God. With God all things are
one and there is no separation between love, life, freedom, power,
wisdom, joy and all the other great and small matters of reality.
But it is necessary for us, who see in part and know in part, to
divide reality into headings. For that which is perfect is not come
and we do not yet see in unity. Love, we may therefore say, is
most significantly the pain-bearer; that which challenges the experience of pain, first in the self and thence in others, and remains
unchanged. In this it does not yield to those reactions by which
evil is caused to proliferate, and thus it is the entire underlying
principle of forgiveness. But, as will be said later on, it is even
more: for if pain is robbed of its power to provoke evil in a
viciously proliferating circle, and if love rules the reactions to it,
then the evil one has been defeated at the heart of his strategy.

Love is the freedom giver. Since freedom is the condition in
which growth takes place and in which love is capable of arising,
the need of freedom is fundamental in the arena of man's endeavour and development. But in the evolutionary dialectic, each
thing contains its own frustration and the seed of its own defeat.
Men and women seek freedom, in psychic ways even more ar-
dently than in physical. In seeking it, one person or one group
puts pressure on another, ignoring or crushing sensitivities; and
one man's freedom too often spells another's constraint or en-
slavement. Freedom falls victim to the selfish quest for freedom.

Only love confers real freedom, because love will bear its own pain in acknowledging another's need and in so doing will evoke the same response in the other. In giving, man finds that he is indeed given unto, just as in forgiving he is forgiven. All things of which love consists appear to have in them the element of pain or a connection with pain. It seems as though in this life love can never be dissociated from pain. Love proves its authenticity by its willingness to face pain and by not turning back at the threat of pain. Therefore love's power is even sharpened, enlarged and deepened by the touch and impact of pain.

To our fragmentary view, love and pain seem to be uneasy bedfellows. Love is often supposed to be a primrose path, the most natural happiness in the world, a thing which may suddenly be grasped round the next corner. Romantic love, the love so often depicted in song, novel and film, is perfectly real and may often seem to be just this natural delightful product of life. But in reality it is only an embryo, or a taste of heaven to set one upon the serious quest of heaven. Love, of the kind of which we have been talking here, lies very far from the pleasant response to emotion and inclination. Human experience at quite ordinary levels confirms this. To love is at many points accompanied of necessity by self-giving and self-sacrifice. This may come in the form of the care, anxiety, responsibility or financial sacrifice of parents in respect of their children; in the day-to-day giving and taking and growing together of marriage relationship; or in the eventual pain of bereavement. At another level, love exercised towards friend or neighbour means the will to do things at one's own inconvenience, to spend time and effort on them, to put oneself at risk physically or emotionally on their behalf. Such things may indeed have to be accomplished by the overcoming of much reluctance or even of natural revulsion. From this there begins to emerge a picture of love which is sufficiently far-reaching to include the possibility, and more likely the probability, of pain and suffering in its exercise. If we say that we have love, and yet if we are not prepared to follow that love through to self-sacrifice and unflinching passing through pain, then we do not truly possess love. It seems that, in the divine wisdom, the love which alone brings man to the fringe of his realized kinship with God is the thing which gives him his greatest vulnerability.

Love was a latecomer. How late can be told from the fact that the Old Testament is, in an important respect, the record of the growing apprehension of love and of the pioneering of its exercise towards God and towards neighbour. It is a story of regular disappointment in the standards perceived or achieved. Still, those standards, expressed through the vision of a few chosen men, grew gradually until the time was ready for the coming of Christ. 'God, who at sundry times and in divers manners spake in time past unto the fathers by the prophets, hath in these last days spoken unto us by his Son' (Hebrews 1.1f.). Not until the incarnation had taken place could love be declared in the fullness of its stature. Even then, even in Christ, it was a fullness which grew only with pain to its perfection.

It might seem obvious that love could not come upon the scene until the human make-up was ready for so refined, vulnerable yet exalted a possession. This is, of course, the case, but it is not the most significant part of the truth. If it were taken as being the main truth, it might indicate that love was a further phase of evolutionary development, leading towards some utopian culmination of the human story. There are writers who have made suggestions of this sort. The consequence of such a position is to obscure the revolutionary nature of love in the evolutionary order and to omit love's central accomplishment of the radical grappling with evil and sin and the conquest of evil at its source. It is the mistake of confusing evolution and salvation.

Far from being the herald of a utopian completion of evolution, love appeared as the intruder on the evolutionary scene. It came not to bring peace but a sword. It came at the time when providence, in the freedom arena of mankind's world, was ready for the second creation. Love heralded the beginning of the end, the dawning of light on the final destiny of man. In that long journey to manhood were to be gathered up and transposed into the substance of the spiritual cosmos the constituents of the embryonic kingdom of God. The long-formed materials of life were to be made raw materials of life. Straw by straw, person by person, attitude by attitude, response by response, instinct by instinct, the motive power of evolution was to be quelled and transformed, restrained and converted into the motive power of spirit. In religious terminology, it was to be redeemed to new uses. Towards this end the whole of the first creation of mineral, vegetable and animal had been pointing. The physical cosmos is the womb and breast and arms which bears, nourishes and sets on its course the second, and spiritual, cosmos. There, in the midst of the creation of which the Word is maker, the Word made flesh strives in the architecting of spiritual man, made also of flesh and yet intended as participant in divine nature.

If love was a latecomer, it was nevertheless also a slow grower. Mankind's entry into love is the crossing of the crucial threshold of his destiny into wider and continually more exacting territory in which love must struggle unceasingly for supremacy.

It is not easy, and perhaps not necessary, to determine how and when the natural potentiality for love, which arose spontaneously in the course of man's psychic and emotional advance, touched the confines of spirituality and became supernaturalized as a partner in God's grace. The borderline between grace and nature is notoriously undiscoverable, the more so now since we have grown out of the mediaeval ideas which depicted grace as an extra 'layer' – like icing on a cake – on the top of nature. Bishop John Robinson's term 'the ground of our being' is a beautiful and a very useful concept to describe that deep level in human nature where the interaction of grace and nature take place. The most that can be said is that the time came when the emergent human spirit began to perceive a spiritual connotation in love and a moral quality expected of it. No doubt the earliest attempts at law and order, as also early instances of worship, were embryos of what would later be realized as obligations of love. Love must have come, as eventually Christ came, almost unperceived.

Much more important to realize is the fact that man's attempt at the practising of love – which we recognize to have been pioneered in particular among the Hebrews – never did and never could reach any degree of perfection by natural growth or by the natural efforts of man's resources. Evolution was not *intended* to lead to perfection. To suppose that it may is for Christians a heresy and for humanists a trail towards disenchantment. Evolution was intended to provide the astonishing psycho-physical being of man with its potentiality now for responding to the Creator and ultimately for sharing the Creator's life and divine nature. Christian doctrine is universally agreed about man's inadequacy to attain to his destined spiritual stature or to obtain righteousness by his own virtues and efforts. The whole story of man's spiritual adventure revolves round his recognition of inability and the corresponding and merciful enablement of divine grace. The sharpness of the frustration which St Paul experienced in his quest for goodness, and which gave such vividness to his doctrine of grace and law, is sign enough of that inadequacy. The evangelical may present the solution to this dilemma principally in the doctrine of justification, while the Catholic may stress the efficacy of sacramental grace, but the situation they are prescribing for is the same. Man's power of spirit could never carry him into spiritual supremacy. That, only Christ could achieve in man's arena and on man's behalf. 'Without me you can do nothing' is experienced truth to every one who sets out on the quest for love. As we look down the long corridor of man's advance and entry into love, we can see that Christ came to do what man was never intended or able to do, to bring creative power to the arena of freedom and there to gain a way of love upon which man might, by divine grace, enter.

That love, which man's resources certainly could not encompass, did not, even in Christ, come into the world as something full-fledged and ready-made. In order to appreciate the depth and reality of the action for which the incarnation took place, it is necessary to be very clear that it was a prodigious creation of something quite new. The sentimental portrayal of Jesus as perfect pattern, divine example-giver both as child and man, distracts attention from essential truths. The reason why the incarnation was no sort of emergency, no act of expediency called forth by man's wickedness, is that the creative task of the Christ was to fashion this new dimension of love which could be formed nowhere else and by no other means than in the arena of man's freedom. He was to make, through his own spirit, will, mind and body, something which had never before existed in the universe, a total supremacy of love amid every change, chance and caprice which freedom might produce.

❧ 14 ❧

Forgiveness and the Defeat of Evil

CHRISTIAN BELIEF has always been drawn towards ascribing to evil an objective reality and an origin in a malign spiritual being, the devil. He has been thought probably to be pre-existent in relation to the world and certainly to be personal and conscious. The present tendency among some thinkers to dismiss the existence of the devil and to explain away the reality of evil must be treated (to say the least) with caution. So far as this chapter is concerned, both aspects of the doctrine are accepted as wholly valid.

In itself evil is invisible, and its purchase upon human motive and will is accomplished invisibly. But its manifestations and realization are inevitably crystallized into fact through the actions and activities of humans in the freedom arena. Mankind, earthbound yet destined for eternity, is the target against whom the devil's evil intentions are directed (as C. S. Lewis so well pointed out in *The Screwtape Letters*). Only in mankind, with human consciousness and will, does there exist the agency for turning those intentions into visible hard fact. Therefore, by the same token, only through mankind can that agency and those intentions be nullified and outflanked. In man alone can the devil be defeated and finally beaten down under our feet. When Jesus talked of seeing Satan fall as lightning from heaven, he was asserting that Satan in his essential spiritual form could have no purchase on the creation until he entered the sphere of mankind's activity. But simultaneously that entry contained the seed of his own defeat in and through man – both Son of Man and son of man.

The processes of growth and the necessary sensitivities built into these processes provided the devil with a great range of vulnerabilities through which, by the threat of pain, man's conduct could be deflected this way and that, and with one all-sufficient and all-efficient weapon by which to bring mankind under his domination (so that the world 'lies in the evil one'). That weapon is pain. The point of purchase on man's motives is the infinitely varied one of man's vulnerability, stretching back into his instinct to survive. If you disentangle the basic motive of every choice of the lesser good or of the greater evil, it will turn out to consist of the avoidance of pain, or the choosing of the marginally less painful.

Equally and on the other side of the coin, to pursue the greater good or to avoid the evil is likely to be achieved at the expense of pain suffered in one or another department of being. It is through the threat of pain that the devil succeeds in deflecting man from his primary duty towards God. Man is quick to feel his liberty threatened by the unknown factor of God's control and demand, and the imagined interference with freedom appears as a basic and unbearable pain. More deeply yet God's moral demand brings with it, in differing degrees, the prospect of that subtle death to self which is a cardinal (and unique) point underlying the Christian idea of conversion and commitment. Those who have embarked on the spiritual endeavour are aware of and still vulnerable to the drawing back which is nature's reaction in face of the fear felt at having yielded up basic control of destiny. This fear is exploited with ease and effect by the devil. It is pain, in one form or another, which deters man from taking the morally higher course (when he perceives that course) in human relations and duty because the way of it is strait and narrow, because it is the line of most resistance, most effort, most self-giving, most risk of rebuff, most fear of failure, most threat of ridicule or a thousand other hurts to pride, body or estate. Equally, it is the dread of pain by which man is lured to take the morally lower course, dictated by inclination or self-interest because it is the way of least resistance, least sacrifice, least discomfort, least cost to self and least confrontation with pain.

It may well be suggested that it is not pain but rather pleasure, lust and desire which do the luring towards the selfish or easier course. While superficially true, this only brings us back to the same answer of pain. The final enticement to fulfil a desire lies in the prospect of pain and deprivation which the rejection of the desire would bring. If I consult myself, I know that to refuse myself something I want means overcoming the pain of decision (plus anger if the desire is strong) and afterwards the pain of actually being without the desired fulfilment. Do we not indeed all know it?

Either way, therefore, whether as deterrent to good or final spur to evil, pain is the chastisement with which the devil is able to bring people to do his bidding.

So much for the devil's *modus operandi*, by which he uses a natural and profound part of human nature – vulnerability to pain – to dominate the conduct of humanity. This underlies his whole strategy, but it is not the whole story. The simple deterrent and the final enticement do not account for the whole or even the most significant part of the evil armoury. They stand as barriers of reluctance and, in the defeat of evil, both have to be overcome. But the real stranglehold of evil over humanity lies in the chain reaction or vicious circle by which, through revenge and misunderstanding and, most of all, through non-forgiveness, pain and sin and sin and pain proliferate and intensify to destroy human relationships and corrupt human hearts. The natural and unregenerate response to receiving a hurt from another person is to return the hurt, by angry words or hurtful deed, upon the person who inflicted it. Mysteriously, that brings a sense of relief of the hurt and makes for a feeling of safety against similar future attacks. Perhaps it is not mysterious or surprising, since the pain and anger have been transferred to the original offender, by way of revenge. But, in fact, the grand total of pain has been increased, a return attack provoked, the relationship further estranged and mutual understanding has perhaps retreated to a point where even the desire to see the other's point of view has disappeared. Hurt feelings, warped judgments and angry reactions ripple outwards to touch and infect other people and the process starts again spreading like an epidemic. There are limitless variations on this theme and all are compounded of the instinctive and impulsive reactions of self-defence and aggression before the threat of diminishment in one way or another. How many relationships, friendships, marriages, even international relations, have been laid in ruins as a result of a progress of events like this?

The long corridor stretching back to our primitive ancestry stands wide open and down it lies a profusion of prides and vulnerabilities which can be stirred and provoked at touch of word, gesture and deed. From this enmeshment in vicious and painful circle there is but one way out. That is by the supernatural power of forgiveness: forgiveness alone can break the chain and hold up the progress of damage upon damage, hurt upon hurt, revenge upon revenge. Forgiveness is the central key piece to that defeat of evil.

Forgiveness is specifically a matter of dealing with pain. If, between two people, there has been no pain, no hurt, no damage, no diminishment inflicted, then there is nothing to forgive. You do not (I think) need to forgive what has not caused you pain. Forgiveness describes the positive, redemptive response to pain, in which, for love's sake, the hurt is contained by refusal to return it with anger and in which love and goodwill are maintained unbroken towards the offender. (There is deep spiritual wisdom in the everyday saying about keeping the door open; though it requires supernatural grace to be able to do so. Apology does not open the door to forgiveness so much as move with a contribution through a door already open.) The original hurt is isolated and so, being contained within the hurt person, is not instrumental in bringing about an increase in the total amount of pain and a consequent proliferation of evil. The original offender is not provoked to renewed offence and the evil is robbed of its power to do further damage. Beneath the surface, a provocation to evil and a potential proliferation into a vicious circle have been overcome by good: a pain sustained has been answered by good will given in return. The originally hurt person has contained and not returned the hurt and so has to continue to feel the suffering of it. However, the motive for so doing is the preservation of relationship for love's sake; and when the supernatural will to love has become entirely dominant over the natural will to take revenge the pain is absorbed – redeemed – in the hurt person and healing flows from that person to the original offender. A pain has been transformed by grace into a source of love for both people. Such is, in brief, the interior anatomy of forgiveness.

If we now look closely at what was happening to Christ and within him, not only during the passion but much earlier in life as well, we shall see that this process, enlarged, deepened, cosmic in scope, is at the heart of the matter. The collect for the Sixth Sunday after the Epiphany says that Christ was manifested that he might destroy the works of the devil. That destruction was accomplished over the issue of pain where the devil might have overcome the sensitivities of the humanity of Christ. There were, over this issue, three times of major confrontation: the wilderness, Gethsemane, the cross. No doubt at all points in his life he trained himself in preparation for the direct confrontation to take whatever buffetings came his way and to pass barriers of inner reluctance in the exercise of love, to risk the consequences of doing right, and, most of all, to retain goodwill against all provocation.

Many issues were fought out in the wilderness; of that there can be no doubt. But the one on which all else hinged and against which the main (and recorded) temptations were directed was the issue of accepting that there could, and must, be no alternative to the confrontation with pain, the weapon with which man was kept in subservience to evil. This was the task for which he had come, and of which the psalms and prophets testified. If Christ had not won through to the perception of this truth, if he had been persuaded to try out superficial remedies which did not touch the main disease, the devil's power would have remained intact, the real enemy would have remained untouched. Stones into bread as a social panacea, spectacular acts to gain public acclaim (and maybe other unrecorded thoughts) were highly alluring because they avoided the entering of the dark stronghold of pain. All might have given temporary acclaim; but the victory would not be for love. Pain would hold its ancient power to provoke evil. The strong man armed would keep his house and his goods would be in peace.

In Gethsemane, Christ was assaulted by the utmost in threat and dread; the devil was exerting his utmost pressure, through the prospect of pain, to deflect Christ from the coming confrontation. The wilderness had established the general determination, but at that time it was still viewed from afar. Now the prospect was at hand and fresh power was necessary for the crucial decision upon which there would be no going back. Grace had to overcome nature's reluctance: the long creative horizon had to outshine the long backward corridor: will, courage and love had to determine that nothing must daunt or deter. If the devil could, even now, place his weapon of pain across the path of Christ to make him stumble and turn back, then his future possession of the souls of men was certain.

On the cross, through the actual pain (and that, of course, not physical only), if the Christ could not bear the price of forgiveness, of meeting pain with love, no one else could. If Christ could be provoked to anger, despair, or revenge, then all men everywhere could be so provoked for ever. On the other hand, if pain failed to deflect Christ and failed to change the content of his love, then the kingdom was open to all believers, the pain which evil inflicted through sin could not close the divine heart. That victory could pass on to be the principle of man's own victory, and the devil's ultimate destruction was assured. Beneath the surface the engagement on which will and spirit and feeling were involved was a struggle in which the devil's power was deployed to its fullest extent. Divine love was drawn forth and deployed similarly to fullest extent. Divine love must meet every device of discouragement which pain could produce, and remain undeflected in the intention to love without anger or resentment. ('The prince of this world . . . has nothing in me.') That love in suffering spells not only whole support and understanding of human suffering in the often gruelling experience of growth towards heaven; it spells the totality of forgiveness of sins, because forgiveness is the love that remains, under every provocation, unchanged towards the offender in order that the offender may be knit together into one again and thus may not die but live.

Beneath the surface of the crucifixion of Christ there is much we do not know; but what we do know is not guesswork, we know it out of the totality of the whole tone of providence. The cross is of one piece with the incarnate life, and the life is of one piece with the whole scheme of the creative growing and becoming in freedom. The incarnation was as essential as the first word which brought the worlds into being; it was the Word which brought eternal man into being. The universe bears passively – mechanically – the hallmark of divine creation. In the spiritual cosmos-chaos of man's freedom, divine love in Christ had to gain supremacy over the wiles of evil expressed in all the hazards and caprices of freedom and in all its pains and sins. From him and from the supremacy of love gained by him there would spread out a spiritual cosmos which would at one and the same time be free – not passive or mechanical – and yet bear the hallmark of divinity. That would be indeed the life of eternity and ultimate heaven. What we know to have gone on during the hours of crucifixion was the battle between the intent of divine creative love and the retrogressive pull goaded by pain to cease, let go, despair, wash the hands, regard the task as impossible, at times perhaps to let the creation sink back into non-being. What broke the heart was not so much sorrow at the world's plight as the sheer moral effort to summon and retain, and settle conclusively for, the undeviating and irrevocable intention to maintain the creative love towards the creation for all time, all people, all human follies. In that lay the source of certainty of mankind's forgiveness and of the devil's defeat. Because such love meant the containing of the pain of mind and body in himself with no relief of returning it upon the perpetrators, present or absent, and no escape by the final temptation to come down from the cross, Christ did take upon himself all the pain of all the sin of all the world.

We have to wrestle with this further question. What happened to the pain thus retained, whether in Christ or in those who follow Christ in forgiving one another? The resurrection of Christ tells that pain and all its associated horrors were not only healed, but were healed because they had been transformed, through the intent to love, from negative to positive (what words does one use?), from darkness to light, from destruction to creation. Not many in any age (I guess) have had really to love their enemies, to love those who falsify truth or who work for deprivation of justice for them, when every fibre of nature, cheered on by the devil, cries for hatred and implacable hatred at that. When that natural venom is fought out of the way and replaced by uncompromising love, a formidable transformation has taken place at cost of formidable sacrificial pain. This surely must go deep into the meaning of atonement and redemption, not as the cancelling of any past event but as the redemptive grasping of an existential spiritual nettle and the quelling of its power to sting.

I love the Prayer of Consecration in the 1662 *Book of Common Prayer*, and I love to use it. But I am uncertain now about the validity of the word satisfaction. Sacrifice is primary because Christ took no alternative way, but bent himself undeterred to the confrontation with pain on which all depended. Oblation is true because it was self-giving, with consent of the will, for the sake of the divine purpose. Satisfaction is different: Christ did not suffer to satisfy either the wrath of God or in such extent as to cancel the sin-content of the whole world, as though weighed in some divine balance. He suffered in such extent, without change of intention, as to prove the divine love to be unalterable in face even of the sin-intractable and pain-bearing of the whole world.[1]

[1] In other words, he did enough – which is what satisfaction means. G.R.D.

If, then, as we may surmise, the crucifixion and resurrection were the key events of the entire unfolding of the creation scheme, and yet were wholly and without doubt parts of that scheme fore-known and foreordained in the divine mind, then some fresh re-flections are cast upon atonement. It has been suggested earlier that the idea of fall should be reinterpreted as the critical phase of development of consciousness when motives and acts of aggression and defence began to be employed for selfish ends with conscious knowledge of their consequences (and therefore of their moral wrongness). There was therefore no primaeval per-fection, no 'primordial tragedy', no forfeiting of God's favour and no wholesale state of alienation.

The atoning sacrifice was neither a rescue operation nor the re-building of a shattered bridge. The divine plan envisaged the inevitability of sin in man's struggle for entry into love (although no single sin is by that fact condoned: 'The Son of Man goeth as it is written of him but woe to that man by whom he is betrayed'). It permitted pain as the deepest necessity of that progress because ultimately love must grow in freedom and be proved and authenti-cated as unshakeable. Pain was for long ages an independent entity unconnected with love. It was essential to progress as 'father of invention', but it thus gave full rein to the vicious circle in which sin and pain complemented one another.

The freedom of the freedom arena of human life was and is very truly and painfully free. In this freedom love had begun to dawn and in its half light man was for ever trying to catch up with and solve the pain problem: pain always looked and looks an alien intruder which it should be possible to stamp out. But the attempt to dodge pain and pursue comfort was apt to produce more pain and more discomfort. Divine providence cannot do without pain as it cannot do without freedom and sin, and life and death, and ultimately love – always in the last issue love. But love which is not reconciled to and proved by pain is not yet love as love is seen in the divine mind. If the writer of Hebrews is right and if the

Christ was 'made perfect by the things which he suffered', then, in the freedom arena where love was on the hazardous journey towards completion, the Logos came, also free and in hazard, to plant the supernatural and uncreated love of the Godhead and establish its supremacy over all that might swamp it. He did many things in support of that love; he shared human status, brought dignity to earthly things, stood by his people in their experience of hazard and pain, and sanctified their enjoyments. Above all these, he brought pain and love together, and out of that seemingly diverse conjunction came the reality of forgiveness. Love is proved in pain, and love comes to its fullest expression in forgiveness which is pain born and transformed into love. Pain no longer has, in principle, independence and need no longer have power to provoke: that it still does so is the measure of what remains of the creation plan to be achieved in man by grace. Forgiveness is also not simply a device for the 'putting right' of what was 'wrong'. Forgiveness does this both between man and man and God and man; but it is the perfecting power within the divine plan, the fulfilment of the divine fore-knowledge, the redeeming of pain, the centre of the spiritual cosmos. In some strange way forgiveness is the healing of the scars of Christ as it should be of the body of Christ. Christ's perfecting lay in the entire yielding to the two major forces of the creative plan, love and pain, so that in him the reconciliation of love and pain constituted his healing.

There is some validity in the verbal symbol at-one-ment, sometimes used to help in the explanation of the doctrine. Christ has brought at-one-ment primarily to the two forces of experience which have most savagely pulled man in two directions, pain and love. In this he has forged the means of at-one-ment between God and man and between man and man where guilt and its consequent barrier have separated them. He has made possible the at-one-ment of mankind's highest aspirations in the pursuit of godliness, past the threats of diminishment and the dreaded death of self. Finally he has, in incarnation and new creation, made a one-ness of the immeasurable separateness of divine and human nature, providing the grace out of his victorious gaining of supremacy of love, by which man, the focus of that one-ness, may enter in the full participation in divine nature in eternity which is the intent of the act of creation.

❧ 15 ❧

The Vindication of God's Honour

TRADITIONAL THEORY has insisted that a part of the atoning act of Christ was to vindicate the honour of God by making towards him on man's behalf an offering in satisfaction for sin, which man could not make in his own person, by means of the 'one oblation of himself once offered'. Nothing could more perfectly state this insistence than the opening of the Prayer of Consecration in the 1662 *Book of Common Prayer*. There is, here, no sense of an impatient deity requiring the smoothing over of his outraged dignity, nor of anger needing to be appeased. The objectivity of the redressing of the balance saves any jarring note. Yet divine impatience and anger have not been far from atonement ideas over the ages.

The vindication of God's honour must centre on his love and the fulfilment of his purpose. There can hardly be vindication for him other than in the assured well-being of his desired creation and in the ultimate victoriousness of his purpose. True, it may be that Christ was offering to God what man could not in his own unperfected person offer. For Christ was indeed offering the thing which no man ever had or ever could have accomplished: the triumph of love undaunted, undeterred and unaltered in face of every potential pain and threat. He was presenting to God the final key piece in the creation puzzle which had to be found in the freedom arena, to the participation of man in the divine life and love, which was the entire purpose of creation: the spiritual gold of forgiveness.

God is vindicated in what happens. Negatively, he is vindicated whenever sin is followed by disaster or unhappiness; positively, when love is seen to heal, forgiveness to rebuild and the divine purpose to go forward. The Old Testament declares this clearly enough in enunciating the divine judgment and mercy. Ultimately, he will be vindicated in the general resurrection. The idea that a balance of offended honour was being redressed seems quite sub-divine in quality of love. At the resurrection of Christ God was proved right: he was vindicated in what happened there. In the establishment of the supremacy of love which gives the assurance that all things work together for good – pain and sin and freedom and forgiveness and love – doubts and resentments can find their solution.

One of the hardest things to accept in the traditional theory and outlook of atonement doctrine has been its insistence on placing man so wholly 'in the doghouse' about all that has gone wrong in the world. God gave man free will – that has always been admitted – and yet in acting part in freedom, part in ignorance or impetuosity, part in stupidity, part in malice and outright sin, part in sheer muddle and doubt, man has had to lay all guilt and blame on himself and grovel over his own wickedness. Hence some of the difficulties attached to deciding exactly what Christ was doing in order to put man right with God and restore him to God's favour. Hence also the ordinary man's problem when he asks why, if God has given freedom and so permitted things to get into a mess, need man bear the whole blame for making the mess? It is a perfectly valid question.

All care must be taken to underline the reality of sin, its painfulness of consequence and its power to bring death, the agony of known guilty alienation from God. All that is always true. But a long look at the process of growing and becoming, at freedom as the sole condition of entry into love, at the deep embeddedness of pain with its defences and aggressions, and then at the transcendently amazing capacities of love with forgiveness as their crown, in fact at the logical harmony of creation and all its parts – this long look enables one to ask another question.

When Christ, in Gethsemane and on the cross, won through

to the ability to say, 'Despite all this and all that has happened and ever could happen, I determine that the divine love in me shall endure undeterred for always towards my creation', then he accomplished the act of forgiveness for the sins and sinfulness of the world. That accomplishment was on mankind's behalf; though whatever is that is also on behalf of the Creator and the love with which he created. But also (in the whole event of the incarnation) Christ the Logos was placing himself in total sharing sympathy with the often gruelling suffering which man encounters in the hazards of growth, and was making plain the divine acknowledgment of the painful toil which the creative purpose places on the human race. Dare we discern anything so outrageous as the idea that here God is making an atonement towards man for all that his desired creation costs man in the making: that he was making love's amends to all those who feel, and have felt, that they cannot forgive God for all the pains which life has foisted, unwanted, upon them? It is certainly true that man, struggling to perceive the justice which his God-like nature demands, cannot forgive God for the fate which freedom's caprice has brought his way. Love in God's fashion is indeed outrageous and a scandal because it does stoop and condescend to what, by lesser standards, it need not. Perhaps God in his love stands, not only as the bestower of forgiveness, but as the Father who, for the sake of the created whose glory is his desire, even stoops to invite the forgiveness he cannot deserve in order to make it one degree easier for man to be drawn into the orbit of love ...